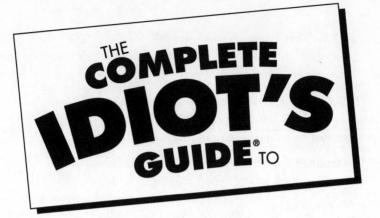

THE COMPLETE IDIOT'S GUIDE® TO

Smoothies

D1052374

by Ellen Brown

ALPHA

A member of Penguin Group (USA) Inc.

For Ilan, Mira, and Tigger, the small folk who add such large joy to my life.

ALPHA BOOKS

Published by the Penguin Group

Penguin Group (USA) Inc., 375 Hudson Street, New York, New York 10014, U.S.A.

Penguin Group (Canada), 10 Alcorn Avenue, Toronto, Ontario, Canada M4V 3B2 (a division of Pearson Penguin Canada Inc.)

Penguin Books Ltd, 80 Strand, London WC2R 0RL, England

Penguin Ireland, 25 St Stephen's Green, Dublin 2, Ireland (a division of Penguin Books Ltd)

Penguin Group (Australia), 250 Camberwell Road, Camberwell, Victoria 3124, Australia (a division of Pearson Australia Group Pty Ltd)

Penguin Books India Pvt Ltd, 11 Community Centre, Panchsheel Park, New Delhi—10 017, India

Penguin Group (NZ), cnr Airborne and Rosedale Roads, Albany, Auckland 1310, New Zealand (a division of Pearson New Zealand Ltd)

Penguin Books (South Africa) (Pty) Ltd, 24 Sturdee Avenue, Rosebank, Johannesburg 2196, South Africa

Penguin Books Ltd, Registered Offices: 80 Strand, London WC2R 0RL, England

Most Alpha books are available at special quantity discounts for bulk purchases for sales promotions, premiums, fund-raising, or educational use. Special books, or book excerpts, can also be created to fit specific needs.

For details, write: Special Markets, Alpha Books, 375 Hudson Street, New York, NY 10014.

Publisher: *Marie Butler-Knight*
Product Manager: *Phil Kitchel*
Senior Managing Editor: *Jennifer Bowles*
Senior Acquisitions Editor: *Renee Wilmeth*
Development Editor: *Christy Wagner*
Production Editor: *Megan Douglass*

Copy Editor: *Nancy Wagner*
Cartoonist: *Chris Eliopoulos*
Cover/Book Designer: *Trina Wurst*
Indexer: *Brad Herriman*
Layout: *Ayanna Lacey*
Proofreading: *Donna Martin*

Contents at a Glance

Contents

6 Low-Fat Smoothies   73

7 Low-Carb Smoothies   89

8 Combo Creations   105

11 Pick-You-Up Smoothies   147

Part 4: Sweet Sensations   161

12 Chocolate Cravings   163

13 Decadent Desserts   177

Introduction

The word *smoothie* always reminds me of a Fred Astaire movie. He glides across the dance floor as if on ice skates, and the only appropriate word to describe him is *smooth*. It's more than grace or rhythm; it's *smooth*.

This image is appropriate to the drink recipes in this book. Smoothies are smooth, as well as being thick and frosty. There's a certain elegance about smoothies that belies how easy they are to make.

I'm not talking about the culinary skills needed to make spun-sugar swans or puff pastry with a hundred layers. I'm talking about measuring the ingredients (and approximately is fine) and looking forward to a drink. If you can press your blender's "On" switch, you can be enjoying a smoothie within minutes.

Smoothies are nothing new. In some shape and form—from malts at an ice cream shop to frozen drinks at a beach bar—smoothies have been around since the invention of the blender some 70 years ago. But certain contemporary lifestyle trends are now making them the national sensation they are today:

- ◆ We are continually reminded of the importance of eating more fresh produce, and, with very few exceptions, all these smoothies have fruit (or in some cases, vegetables) as their base.

- ◆ As the medical community reveals more about the potential hazards of saturated fat and trans-fatty acids, we are looking for ways to incorporate protein into our diets without these risks. With a little forethought, smoothies can qualify as low- or no-fat treats. And for even more nutrition, we can add soy foods and nutritional supplements.

- ◆ We're a nation that eats while driving and for whom convenience is key. Smoothies are a meal we can sip safely. They're the ultimate in "car cuisine."

- ◆ We're beginning to exercise more, and we're turning talking about exercise into actually doing it. As you'll see in Chapter 10, you can formulate smoothies to replenish all the vital nutrients you expend working out.

Although smoothies do meet nutritional needs, the recipes in this book are not medicine; they're drinks. And I hope you'll find them delicious drinks. There are references in Chapter 2 and Chapter 3 to specific nutritional strengths of different foods, but these recipes were invented for their flavor.

There's another trend in contemporary society met by smoothies: we want food that tastes good, and we really don't care that it's good for us. Smoothies do both.

How This Book Is Organized

The book is divided into four parts:

Part 1, "A Smoothie Is a Smoothie Is a Smoothie ..." makes you a smoothie master. It details the basic procedure for making all smoothies, including how to best select and use a blender. It then presents biographies of the most common smoothie ingredients. You'll find a wide range of fresh and frozen fruits, along with dairy products, protein-rich soy foods, and a few representatives from the vegetable patch. You'll also learn a number of ways to dress up smoothies with garnishes.

Part 2, "Fantastic Fruits (and Veggies) for Every Diet," gives you scores of ways to use fruits and juices in your smoothies. The recipes are divided by the nutritional profile of the ingredients other than fruits. There are chapters for smoothies made with dairy products, made without dairy products, low-fat smoothies, and (relatively) low-carb smoothies. Part 2 ends with a chapter of recipes that highlight vegetables and herbs along with fruits.

Part 3, "Smoothies with a Kick," offers a collection of smoothies with nutritional extras. Here you'll find recipes with additives such as protein powder or bee pollen so you can slip the nutrition past your children, who will think they're just drinking smoothies based on ingredients they love. In another chapter, the recipes are intended to replenish vital nutrients, such as potassium, that are lost during strenuous exercise. Part 3 ends with a chapter of smoothies based on liquids that are high in caffeine and can give you an energy boost.

Part 4, "Sweet Sensations," proves that it's always prudent to eat your vegetables so you can then have dessert. You can drink all these desserts, and some are similar to the malts and frappés of my (and maybe your) youth. One chapter covers delicious chocolate smoothies and another equally luscious smoothies without chocolate. The last chapter is for adults only and has alcohol-based recipes that can double as cocktails or after-dinner drinks.

At the end, you'll find some useful appendixes. A glossary will add to your knowledge of cooking lingo, and an appendix of charts will help you convert measurements to the metric system.

Extras

In every chapter, you'll find many boxes that give you extra information to ensure that your smoothies will always be super or to expand your knowledge of food and cooking.

Smooth Sailing

These boxes are cooking tips. Some are specific to the recipes they accompany; others will boost your general cooking skills or give you ideas for presentation. They are meant to make your life easier and make your time in the kitchen more pleasurable.

Ellen on Edibles

Cooking has a language all its own, and some of the terms and ingredients can be intimidating if you don't know what they mean. These boxes are ingredient definitions, and a collection of them is then compiled in a glossary at the end of the book.

Blender Beware

Smoothie recipes are all easy, but it's always a good idea to be alerted to potential problems in advance. These boxes provide just such warnings, either about the entire recipe or a specific ingredient included.

Nutritional Analysis

All the recipes in this book have been annotated with some nutritional information so you know what you're drinking. Because these recipes are meant as food and not as medicine, the analysis does not detail every mineral or vitamin. It does provide you with some useful information, though, especially if you're eating a diet low in fat or low in carbohydrates.

Acknowledgments

Writing a book is a solitary endeavor, but its publication is always a team effort. My thanks go to …

Renee Wilmeth of Alpha Books and Gene Brissie of James Peters Associates for proposing the project.

Christy Wagner, Megan Douglass, and Nancy Wagner for their expert and eagle-eyed editing.

Joan Clark for her insights into nutrition as well as accurate nutritional analysis of the recipes.

Karen Berman for her expert critique and guidance as a technical editor.

Tigger-Cat Brown, my furry companion, who kept me company for endless hours at the computer and approved all dairy recipes.

Special Thanks to the Technical Reviewer

The technical reviewer for *The Complete Idiot's Guide to Smoothies* was Karen Berman, a Connecticut-based writer and editor who specializes in food and culture. She is a contributing editor to *Wine Enthusiast* magazine, and her work has appeared in magazines, newspapers, and newsletters. She is the author of an illustrated history book, *American Indian Traditions and Ceremonies*, and she has worked in various editorial capacities on numerous cookbooks.

Trademarks

All terms mentioned in this book that are known to be or are suspected of being trademarks or service marks have been appropriately capitalized. Alpha Books and Penguin Group (USA) Inc. cannot attest to the accuracy of this information. Use of a term in this book should not be regarded as affecting the validity of any trademark or service mark.

A Smoothie Is a Smoothie Is a Smoothie ...

This part can be called "Anatomy of a Smoothie." Or you might consider it "Everything You Ever Wanted to Know About a Smoothie But Were Afraid to Ask." Smoothies are not rocket science. They are easy recipes that produce delicious results.

In Part 1, you learn the best way to use your blender—and what to look for when you go blender shopping if you don't already have one. The chapters in Part 1 list all the ingredients commonly included in smoothies, from a cornucopia of fresh (or frozen) fruits (and even a few vegetables) to creamy dairy products, protein-rich soy foods, and other alternatives.

You also learn how to dress up a smoothie with some easy garnishes, should you choose.

Chapter

1

How to Build a Smoothie

In This Chapter

- ◆ Defining a smoothie
- ◆ Component parts
- ◆ Selecting a blender or smoothie maker
- ◆ Blender basics

If you can press a button, you can be drinking a thick and luscious smoothie any time of day.

Smoothies have been around since the 1930s, when the first blender was invented and owners started experimenting by whirring up some fruit with ice. As early as the 1950s, West Coast health food stores were selling thick puréed fruit drinks. The term *smoothie* was first used in a blender cookbook in the early 1960s, and since then, the drink has spread in popularity from the California beaches across the nation, especially during the past decade—and with good reason. Smoothies are easy, good for you, and portable—perfect for today's on-the-go society.

In this chapter, you learn how to build a smoothie, starting with a basic definition of what a smoothie is. You'll then learn what different categories of foods go into smoothies. Then, to round out your new-found knowledge of all things smoothie, I give you some information on the essential piece of kitchen equipment you'll need to make smoothies—a blender.

Smoothie Savvy

What is a smoothie? In this book, we'll work with the definition that a smoothie is a thick, frosty drink made with liquids and solids in a blender. As you'll see later in this chapter, which ingredients fall in the "liquid" and "solid" categories can vary greatly. If you can drink it from a glass, but it's so thick you could also eat it with a spoon, it's a smoothie.

Car Cuisine

Because smoothies are served in a cup, they're great candidates for portable sipping while you're riding the subway to work or driving the kids to school. Although smoothies can be a refreshing treat any time of day, they're on the top of the list as a healthful breakfast. (Plus, it's a lot safer to sip a smoothie behind the wheel than attempt to eat a bowl of cereal.)

A Little of This, a Little of That

Making smoothies isn't rocket science. You can personalize smoothies in myriad ways. You can use skim milk in place of whole milk, or you can indulge yourself and make a smoothie richer with ice cream rather than frozen yogurt. Almost anything you add to personalize a recipe will be good.

Blender Beware

When making modifications in a smoothie recipe, be sure the substitutions are within the same category of ingredient. For example, it's fine to substitute frozen yogurt for ice cream but not to substitute frozen yogurt for the fruit amount listed in the recipe.

If you need some help thinking of variations on the recipes here, or like a particular recipe but want to spice it up a notch, I'll give you some tips on ways to change the basic smoothie at the end of the recipes.

You'll notice that almost all the recipes are written for two servings.

You can either cut the recipes in half, if making it just for yourself, or you can enjoy half immediately and place the other half in the freezer for a future smoothie treat.

If frozen, the smoothie needs to partially defrost, at which time it can be placed back in the blender and whirred to a creamy consistency.

Anatomy of a Smoothie

There are only a few categories of ingredients that go into a smoothie. You need something solid to make it thick, something liquid to make it drinkable, and something to bind it together to make it *emulsified*.

Ellen on Edibles

Remember how your chemistry teacher defined an **emulsion?** Two distinct molecules that combine to form a new one. In cooking, an emulsion is similar: Two distinct ingredients combine to form a new mixture that stays together. The key is in the combining. In a salad dressing, the oil automatically rises above the water until you shake the dressing to emulsify it. In a smoothie, the blender's beating action emulsifies the ingredients, and the emulsion stays together because one ingredient binds to the others.

The Essential Solid

One hallmark of a smoothie is its thick texture. Most of the time the thickness comes from *puréed* fruit. The higher the water content in the fruit, the less texture the fruit adds to the drink. For example, a banana, a solid with creamy texture and a low water content, will make a smoothie far thicker than cubes of watermelon will. Watermelon is more than 90 percent water, so once it's puréed, you have a lot of pink water without much texture.

The amount of fiber in a fruit also determines how much texture it adds to the smoothie. Pineapple, for example, has a significant water

Ellen on Edibles

Purée is both a verb and a noun. To purée is to reduce a food to a thick, creamy texture, usually using a blender or food processor. A purée is what you pour out of the blender or food processor.

content, but it has more fiber than, say, peaches, so it will add more body to the drink.

In addition to fruits, the "solid" component of the smoothie equation can also be vegetables, nuts, chocolate, or ice cubes or frozen juice cubes.

Liquids for Luster

In addition to a solid, you have to have a liquid in the blender to make a smoothie something you can drink from a glass rather than eat with a spoon from a bowl.

As with the variety of solids you can use, any number of liquids, starting with various milks—from cows or soybeans—or fruit juices, brewed drinks such as coffee and tea, reconstituted drink powders, or wine or liquor.

The Benefits of Binders

Some fruits, such as bananas, give smoothies a creamy texture, but most often this role is played by the *binder*. Sometimes called a liaison, a binder can be a dairy product, such as yogurt, frozen yogurt, or ice cream. Binders can also be nondairy, such as silken tofu or frozen tofu. Certain nutritional supplements, such as soy protein powder, can also serve as binders.

Ellen on Edibles

A **binder** is an ingredient that makes the final recipe product thick. Classic French sauces, for example, use ingredients such as egg yolks or a mixture of flour and liquid or fat as binders. For smoothies, the binder is usually a thick, creamy product that can be refrigerated or frozen, although certain fruits, such as bananas, can be binders, too.

Personalized Procedure

There's only one actual rule for smoothie-making: Because smoothies are always enjoyed chilled, some of the ingredients should be frozen, but not all of them, or you'll end up with a snow cone rather than a smoothie. One ingredient should always be liquid (or in the case of yogurt or silken tofu, a soft, creamy solid); however, the percentage of frozen ingredients you use determines the texture of your smoothie. The more frozen ingredients, the thicker the texture; the fewer frozen ingredients, the thinner the texture.

For example, let's say you're making a smoothie with 1 banana, 1 cup yogurt, and ½ cup orange juice. If you use a banana you sliced and froze a few days ago with the yogurt and orange juice you just pulled out of the refrigerator, you'll end up with a nice, thick smoothie.

But if you grab a room-temperature banana from the kitchen table, throw in a few orange juice ice cubes to get that same good texture you'd get with a frozen banana.

If you like really chilled and really thick smoothies, use more frozen ingredients. If you like the drink only slightly thicker than a glass of juice, then use all your ingredients right from the refrigerator.

> **Smooth Sailing** _____
>
> You can always tell a smoothie devotee by opening his or her freezer and spotting bags of fruit juice ice cubes. If you're a smoothie lover or want to be one, freeze orange juice and apple juice cubes ahead of time, and you're halfway to a smoothie. (You can measure the capacity of your ice cube tray by filling one hole with a measuring spoon.)

In Order, Please

When you look at the recipes in this book, you'll notice that they all call for the liquid and soft ingredients to be blended first and then the frozen ingredients incorporated. There's a reason for this: Even the most powerful blender will take a long time to crush frozen ingredients. The blending will work much better if there's a liquid base to keep the frozen ingredients moving inside the blender jar.

If you're using ingredients in a different form than those listed in the recipe, reverse the order of use. For example, if you're using a frozen banana rather than one at room temperature, add it at the end of the recipe rather than at the beginning. Remember: frozen ingredients go last.

Choose Your Weapon

Chances are you already own a blender. It might be in the basement along with your high school yearbooks, but a few years ago you had a craving for a frozen margarita, so you bought one. If that's the case, dust it off, and you're all set.

If you're buying a new one, you don't have to mortgage the house to purchase the Rolls Royce of blenders to create delicious smoothies. When blender shopping, look for a blender that has ...

- **A heavy base.** The base stabilizes the machine and keeps it from jumping around on the counter. Pick up blenders when you're shopping to determine which ones feel heavier.

- **A strong motor.** Heavy-duty motors of 60 hertz or more are strong enough for chopping ice, and they'll last far longer than machines with less power.

- **A glass jar.** You might think plastic is more practical, especially if you have young children running around, but plastic scratches over time, and many plastic jars are not dishwasher-safe. Some of the most expensive blenders have stainless-steel jars. They are the most durable, yes, but you can't see what's going on inside.

- **A large-capacity jar.** Find a blender with a 40-ounce-capacity jar. Remember, ingredients in a blender need room to move around. A 40-ounce jar is enough for a smoothie for 2 or 3 people.

- **A two-piece lid.** The lid should fit very snugly on the jar to avoid leaks. That part is essential. It's also nice if there's a small access hole in the center of the lid that you can remove to add ingredients when the machine is running.

- **Variable speeds.** As long as you have high and low, you're set. The blenders with numerous buttons across the front are not really necessary for making smoothies. It's also nice if you can pulse the blender on and off rather than turning it on full-blast. This allows you to incorporate ingredients without turning them into a purée.

◆ **A pleasing appearance.** This does not affect performance, but it can be important. Blenders range from simple to sleek, and how much appearance matters is purely up to you. All blenders do the same job. If you're going to leave it out on the counter, you might want to buy one you find aesthetically pleasing or that matches your other counter appliances.

> **Smooth Sailing**
> When you're blender shopping, consider how easy or inexpensive it will be to replace the jar or purchase a second jar. It could make the difference between two machines at a similar price point.

Blender by Another Name

The new kid on the blender block is called a smoothie maker. Smoothie makers are—you guessed it—designed specifically for making smoothies and look much like blenders but have a higher base.

Why the higher base? The jar has a spigot at the bottom from which you dispense the completed smoothie. Because you dispense with the machine running at low speed, the liquid is forced into the glass, regardless of how thick it might be.

Smoothie makers are handy, and most are priced comparably to middle-of-the-road blenders. However, the smoothie maker's higher base might not fit in or under a cabinet as easily as a conventional blender.

Food Processor Foibles

Food processors are a boon for almost all categories of food preparation, but they are not as effective for smoothie-making as a blender or smoothie maker. They don't crush ice or incorporate other frozen ingredients as well as a blender. The large blades are the wrong shape,

> **Smooth Sailing**
> If you're using a food processor, crush the ice in advance by placing it in a heavy plastic bag. Pound it with the back of a small pot until the chunks are no larger than lima beans.

and the overall shape of the work bowl does not aerate the smoothie mixture to create the characteristic creamy texture.

Blender 101

A blender might look innocuous enough, but it's definitely a machine you need to approach with caution. These usage tips will help you get the most from your blender:

- Always keep one hand on the top of the lid to ensure it won't fly off.
- Turn off the blender completely before removing the lid, and allow the liquid to stop moving.
- Never put your hands in the blender jar, and be sure the blades have stopped moving before you insert a spatula into the jar.
- Use only rubber spatulas, not metal spoons or knives.
- Cut food that will go into the blender into small, uniform-size pieces. An ice cube is about the largest-size object you should add to the blender.
- Never fill a blender more than two thirds full. When the motor moves the liquid around, it will push it above the level of the ingredients at rest. Never fill it too full, or you could have a mess.

Keeping It Clean

Always unplug the power cord from the outlet before you clean the blender's base, and even if you've just spilled a bottle of chocolate syrup all over it, never immerse the base in water. Just use a lot of soapy rags or paper towels to get it clean.

Every few times you use the blender—or each time if you blend foods such as raw eggs or meats that could be carrying bacteria—it's a good idea to disassemble the base from the jar and clean all the parts separately.

If the jar is dishwasher-safe, it can be disassembled and washed with the blades and cap in the silverware basket and the jar upright. However, do not wash the rubber gasket in the dishwasher since the hot water in the washing cycle and high heat of the drying cycle will crack the rubber.

For an interim cleaning, rinse out the jar well under hot water. Then add a teaspoon dishwashing liquid to the jar, and fill it half full with water. Pulse on low speed a few times to clean the interior and blades well.

The Least You Need to Know

- Smoothies are thick, cold drinks made in a blender or a smoothie maker (food processors don't work as well).
- Smoothies only need three basic ingredients: a solid, a liquid, and a binder.
- The texture of smoothies varies, depending on the percentage of frozen ingredients to liquid.
- Your blender is easy to clean, but never immerse the power base in water.

Chapter 2

Fruits (and Veggies) for All Seasons

In This Chapter

- ◆ Fruit-freezing basics
- ◆ Tree-ripened fruits
- ◆ A bowl full of luscious berries
- ◆ Treats from the tropics
- ◆ Vine-ripened melons
- ◆ A few vegetables for good measure

When many people think *smoothie*, their first thought is *fruit*. Fruit is as natural in smoothies as it is healthful. Check out a food pyramid dietary guide or talk to a nutritionist, and you'll see just what part fruit plays in a good diet. And luckily, smoothies are a great way to increase the number of fruit servings in your diet.

In this chapter, I give you a guide to the fruits best and most often used to make smoothies. You'll learn how to tell if fruits are ripe and ready for blending and how to freeze ripe fruit for future treats.

In addition, because some veggies are as good in smoothies as fruits are, I also discuss some vegetables that are included in recipes later in this book.

Fresh from the Freezer

There's nothing like the flavor and aroma of fresh fruit, but if you don't have any fresh fruit in your kitchen when a smoothie craving hits, it's better to use *dry-packed frozen fruit* rather than canned fruit or unripe fruit. Frozen fruits are picked and frozen at the peak of ripeness, and for making smoothies, they save time without sacrificing flavor.

Ellen on Edibles

Dry-packed frozen fruits are frozen in individual pieces without any syrup or additional sugar. You'll find the fruits in plastic bags in the freezer section of your supermarket.

Modern air transportation has given us a new definition of "airline food," and we can now enjoy almost all fruits year-round thanks to air freight from other countries—but we do pay a price for this convenience. If you stock up on fruits when they are either in season locally or attractively priced and then freeze them yourself, you'll save money, plus have a freezer stocked with smoothie-making fruit whenever you want it.

The best way to freeze fruit is to first prepare the fruit by cleaning, slicing, peeling, sectioning, etc., as appropriate—I give you specific information for fruit preparation later in this chapter. Then simply arrange ½- to 1-inch pieces on a baking sheet covered with plastic wrap and put them into the freezer until they're frozen. Once frozen, transfer the fruit to a heavy, resealable plastic bag. Mark the date on the bag, and use the fruit within 2 months.

Tree-Ripened Treats

Versatile bananas, apples, and oranges are available year-round at a reasonable cost and work well in smoothies. Fruits such as peaches and plums are best used in their season. You'll see the following fruits used in the recipes in this book:

◆ **Apples.** Although not as high in vitamins as some other fruits, apples do contain a high level of pectin, which helps reduce cholesterol. Always available and ripe, there's no reason to freeze apples. But if you want to freeze them to make your smoothie thicker, first toss them with fresh lemon juice after slicing to prevent discoloration.

◆ **Apricots.** High in beta-carotene, which the body converts to vitamin A, pale ripe apricots are also a good source of fiber and potassium. A ripe apricot is soft when gently pressed, and the skin is thin enough that it does not have to be peeled. Just slice the apricot and discard the pit.

Smooth Sailing

Almost any fruit that can be frozen whole or in pieces can also be frozen as a purée. Cut it into small chunks and place it in the blender with some water or juice. Blend until puréed; then freeze the purée in ice cube trays. Transfer the cubes to a heavy plastic bag once frozen. The cubes will give your smoothies a vivid flavor and thick texture.

◆ **Cherries.** Rich in potassium and B vitamins, sweet cherries come in a range of colors and they all make great smoothies. Discard the stems, rinse the cherries in a colander, cut them in half and discard the pits, and they're ready to go. They can also be successfully frozen after they're prepared this way.

◆ **Grapes.** Both green and red grapes are high in potassium, and their flavor is almost identical. Which one you choose depends on your aesthetic preference and which one seems the sweetest. Rinse and remove the grapes from the stems; then dry on paper towels. You can freeze them without any slicing or dicing.

Blender Beware

You'll most often find Thompson seedless grapes in markets, but do beware of grapes with seeds when you're shopping for smoothie ingredients. Slicing the grapes in half and removing the seeds is time-consuming, and if you miss any seeds, they'll add a bitter taste to smoothies, even if well puréed.

♦ **Oranges.** Oranges are a superb source of vitamin C. Seedless navel oranges are always in season and are the ideal choice for smoothies. The best way to prepare oranges is to cut off the top and bottom so the orange will sit snugly on the work surface. Then use a serrated fruit knife to cut off the peel, including the white pith. Cut between the white lines that mark the sections, and the orange sections, sans peel, will pop right out.

♦ **Peaches.** Like other orange-fleshed fruits, peaches are an excellent source of beta-carotene. Peaches are ripe if they're soft when pressed gently. Whether or not you want to peel the peaches is a personal decision. But if you choose not to, even after a long time in the blender, bits of peel will still be in your smoothie. If you prefer peeled peaches, drop them into boiling water for 30 seconds, remove and drain lightly, and the skins will slip right off when you rub the fruit. You can also use frozen peach slices that are already peeled.

> **Smooth Sailing**
>
> There are two basic types of peaches, clingstone and freestone. They taste similar, and the only difference is whether or not the flesh clings to the pit. Both make an excellent smoothie, and regardless of which you pick, choose the ripest peach you can find.

♦ **Pears.** Fiber-rich pears are a good source of vitamin C and potassium. Pears ripen better off the tree, and it might take up to a week for them to ripen if they're rock-hard when you buy them. You can substitute any variety of pear for another, but peel whichever pear you choose with a vegetable peeler before you use it. Toss pear slices with lemon juice to prevent discoloration. Pears do not freeze well, and canned pears packed in juice are a better alternative if ripe fresh pears are unavailable.

> **Smooth Sailing**
>
> Plums have a crease on one side that runs parallel to the flat side of the pit. Slice plums lengthwise along the crease, and you should be able to see the pit. Discard it, and you're ready to slice or dice.

♦ **Plums.** Rich in antioxidant vitamin C, all the hundreds of species of plums are good in smoothies if they're ripe. You can tell a plum is ripe if it's soft when you gently press it with your finger. Just rinse plums before slicing them, and discard the pit. Peeling is not necessary.

It's the Berries

The bright color and intense flavor of various berries make them popular fruits for smoothies. They marry well with other fruits, ranging from creamy bananas to fragrant pineapple. You'll find these berries in the recipes in this book:

- **Blackberries.** Blackberries, rich, purple-black in color and high in heart-healthy compounds called saponins, are actually a cluster of tiny fruits, each with its own seed. They're most common and affordable during the summer and can be successfully frozen after a quick rinse and gentle patting with paper towels.

- **Blueberries.** In addition to antioxidant vitamins, blueberries are high in salicylate, a compound that reduces inflammation. Look for berries that are plump, not shriveled, and have a slight grayish patina. Rinse them, discard any stems, twigs, or small green berries, and they're ready to go. You can use blueberries fresh, or dry them on paper towels and freeze them in a plastic bag.

- **Cranberries.** It's not a wives' tale: Cranberries, high in vitamin C, do alleviate bladder infections because they prevent bacteria from attaching to the wall of the bladder. Select plump, nonshriveled cranberries and rinse them in a colander. It's difficult to find fresh cranberries except in the fall, so buy a few extra bags when you can find them and freeze them for use during the year by rinsing them and placing them in plastic bags.

Blender Beware

Because it can be quite acidic, most bottled cranberry juice is either sweetened with corn syrup or other sweeteners or blended with apple or grape juices (often there's less cranberry in it than other juice). If you want real cranberry flavor, look for the real thing sold by smaller brands and in health food stores. It might need sweetening, but it's worth it.

- **Raspberries.** Vitamin C is the big boast of succulent raspberries, which are now grown in a rainbow of colors, from classic red to golden amber. When choosing fresh raspberries, look at the bottom of the container, and choose one that has the least amount of juice. That's a sign that the berries are not damaged or moldy.

Smooth Sailing

A blender will create a smooth texture, but sometimes small bits such as strawberry or raspberry seeds will still be visible. If you want these removed, it only takes a few seconds to push the blended smoothie through a fine-meshed strainer.

Ellen on Edibles

Fraises du bois literally means "strawberries of the woods" in French, and you can find these tiny treats in specialty produce markets, most often in the spring. Treat them as you would any other berry.

Place berries in a bowl of water, and stir them around to dislodge any lingering dirt. Then gently pat them dry on paper towels. You can also buy bags of frozen raspberries.

♦ **Strawberries.** A good source of iron as well as B vitamins and vitamin C, strawberries do not ripen once they've been picked, so what you buy is what you get. Because most companies "top dress" the packages with the "hero berries" on the top, check out the bottom of the package when you're buying fresh. Generally, the smaller the berry, the more intense the flavor. Tiny European *fraises du bois* are the sweetest of all. Rinse the berries, and cut off the caps just prior to blending them. They can be frozen after a quick rinse and the caps trimmed, too.

Tropical Treats

Bananas have been imported for almost a century, but finding other aromatic and flavorful fruits from the tropics is a relatively new phenomenon on the North American mainland. These will add punch to your purée when making a smoothie:

♦ **Bananas.** Bananas are an easy way to get a creamy smoothie without adding cream—or any binder, for that matter. They are a fantastic source of potassium, an electrolyte lost during exercise, as well as an excellent source of magnesium and vitamin B_6. Bananas are truly ripe when the peels are mottled with brown spots, not just bright yellow. Once truly ripe, use them sliced fresh, or slice them into ½-inch slices and freeze them.

♦ **Mangoes.** Like other orange-fleshed fruits, mangoes are a good choice for beta-carotene. Mangoes are ripe if they're slightly soft when pressed and the skin is mottled with red and orange. Avoid buying rock-hard green mangoes because they might never ripen. Once peeled and diced, mango cubes can be frozen and placed in a plastic bag.

Smooth Sailing

Mangoes have a hard way and an easy way of being peeled, and it varies fruit to fruit. If you're having problems cutting away the skin, try peeling it from the other end. The stone (pit) is elliptical, and once you've determined its shape, cut a parallel cut on both sides to remove as much flesh as possible, then cut off any flesh remaining on the stone.

♦ **Papayas.** Nutritionally, papaya is best known as a source of the enzyme *papain*. Papayas should be somewhat soft and golden orange when you buy them. If the fruit is hard, cut a small slice off both ends, then make a few lengthwise cuts into the flesh. The papaya will ripen in a few days at room temperature. Always peel the papaya and discard the peppery seeds before cubing it. Once peeled and diced, papaya cubes can be frozen and placed in a plastic bag.

Ellen on Edibles

Papain is an enzyme that can ease indigestion and has been shown to protect the stomach from ulcers. It is also a tenderizer, so save papaya skins and toss them into a meat marinade to speed along tenderizing meats.

♦ **Pineapples.** Pineapples are a good source of minerals, including potassium, calcium, iron, and iodine. Choose one that is fragrant and plump with an overall golden color, or allow it to sit at room temperature until it meets that description. Slice off the top and bottom so it sits flat on your work surface. Then, with a strong knife, slice off the peel. Slice the pineapple in half, and make a

V-shape cut to remove the tough core. Then slice it into cubes. Pineapple cubes can be frozen and placed in a plastic bag.

Make Mine Melon

Melons are low in calories and high in flavor. When melon shopping, choose melons that are heavy for their size. This weight means they are filled with juice.

Melon performance in smoothies varies by species. Watermelon becomes just slightly thicker water, while honeydew becomes a creamy binder.

Freezing melon is not recommended, as it tends to diminish the subtle flavors. Melons are now available year-round, so it's not really necessary to freeze them.

Here is an overview of the most popular melons for smoothies:

◆ **Cantaloupes.** Cantaloupes are rich in beta-carotene, vitamin C, and potassium. The rind should appear well netted. To tell if it was picked ripe, look at the stem end. It should be a full scar, without flesh attached, showing that it was picked when mature. Cantaloupe can be a carrier of salmonella, so wash the rind with soap and water before peeling it. Discard the seeds and cut the flesh into cubes.

Smooth Sailing

Melons are the juiciest of fruits, and some of the juice can be lost when you're peeling and removing the seeds. Always handle melons over a mixing bowl to catch the sweet juice. Then strain the juice and toss it into the blender along with the fruit.

◆ **Honeydews.** A good source of both potassium and vitamin C, the dense flesh of honeydew melons gives smoothies a creamy texture. Choose ones that are green, not white, and slightly perfumed. Cut honeydew melons into quarters and then cut away the soft flesh from the hard peel. Because the fruit is puréed in smoothies, how pretty it looks is irrelevant.

◆ **Watermelons.** Watermelons are rich in electrolytes, which makes them a good choice for a snack after a strenuous workout or any other time you might be dehydrated. One of the great feats of genetic engineering is the seedless watermelon. They're not as much fun because you can't spit the seeds at your friends, but they're much easier for making a smoothie. It's easier to cut the flesh off the rind after cutting a watermelon in quarters than it is to cut through the rock-hard rind. Discard the seeds, if necessary, and cut the melon into cubes.

Versatile Veggies

Vegetables are low in calories and high in nutrients. They create smoothies that blend savory and sweet when combined with fruits. We'll use these veggies in the recipes in this book:

◆ **Carrots.** It's no wonder our parents were always pushing carrots on us. They're a nutritional powerhouse, and their innately sweet flavor makes them compatible with fruits in a smoothie. Choose carrots that are not cracked, and avoid ones with a green tinge at the top, which indicates that the carrot was sunburned and could be bitter. There's really no need to peel carrots if you scrub them well with a vegetable brush. Carrot slices can be frozen, but it's not recommended because some of the sweetness can be lost.

> **Blender Beware**
>
> Although you might think you'll be adding some extra nutrients by using the green carrot tops, always discard the greens, even if you're putting them through a juice machine. Carrot foliage contains toxic substances and is inedible—unless you're a rabbit.

◆ **Cucumbers.** The mild taste of cucumbers makes them a foil for more dominant flavors in a smoothie. They also are compatible with a number of fresh herbs. Always peel waxed cucumbers, but organic or English cucumbers with thin skin can just be rinsed well and used as is. The cucumber skin is a source of the mineral silica, which is good for connective tissue and your complexion.

Whether or not to discard the seeds is a personal decision. If the cucumber is large, the seeds can be hard and do not pulverize well in the blender. But if you don't mind the textural problem, they don't add any bitter flavor.

◆ **Tomatoes.** Botanists classify tomatoes as a fruit, but I'm listing them in the vegetable section because we eat them as a vegetable. Today's science touts tomatoes for their lycopene content, which is proven to have anti-cancer qualities. In addition, they contain a good amount of vitamin C and potassium. There's nothing like a vine-ripened tomato fresh from the garden. Second to that, choose ones at the market that don't have ridges at the stem end, which is a sign the tomato might be mealy. Canned peeled tomatoes are fine to use in a smoothie and might even have more flavor than immature winter ones. Once cored and cubed, tomatoes freeze very well. But do not substitute sun-dried tomatoes, because they are very strong in flavor.

> **Smooth Sailing**
>
> Tomato skin is thin and grinds up well in the blender. But if you want a super-smooth smoothie, peel the tomatoes first. With a sharp knife, cut an X in the bottom of each tomato, then drop them into boiling water for 30 seconds. Drain, and when the tomato is cool enough to handle, the skins will slip right off.

The Least You Need to Know

◆ Most fruits can be frozen in cubes or whole to make smoothies.

◆ Fruits should be used within a few months of freezing to preserve the best flavor.

◆ Bananas and honeydew melons add a creamy texture to smoothies without using a dairy product.

◆ If a melon is heavy for its size, you know it'll be juicy and good for smoothie-making.

◆ Orange-fleshed fruits such as peaches and mangoes are good sources of beta-carotene.

◆ Tomatoes contain lycopene, which has been shown to have anti-cancer qualities.

3

Enhancing Extras

In This Chapter

- ◆ Dairy products for creamy smoothies
- ◆ The world of nutritious soy foods
- ◆ Nutritional supplements that make a smoothie a meal
- ◆ Easy garnishes for dressing up your drinks

Fruits are the stars of smoothies, but as in every recipe, you also need supporting players. In this chapter, you learn what your options are for those "extra" ingredients.

Smoothies made with dairy products and many nondairy products are similar in texture, so depending on your desired diet, you can vary the liquid ingredient. I give you a few ideas in this chapter.

If you want to add a little extra nutritional kick to your smoothie, you learn which nutritional supplements can be best masked by the vivid flavors of smoothies.

And finally, because smoothies are thick, you easily can make a number of garnishes and float them on top of your smoothie for some dressed-up fun. Those tips and ideas are in this chapter, too.

Dairy Delights

Many children of all ages have been lured into eating fruit when it was blended with some ice cream, and part of what gives a smoothie its creamy texture is the dairy ingredient. From milk to ice cream to yogurt, you have several dairy options. Even skim milk will work, as it has a creamy texture.

When making a smoothie, you can use any dairy product interchangeably with another as long as the flavors are consistent. For example, if you want to increase the *acidophilus* in your diet, use vanilla yogurt in place of vanilla frozen yogurt or vanilla ice cream.

Ellen on Edibles

Acidophilus, an ingredient used to thicken yogurt, is a friendly bacteria, called a "probiotic" in some natural food circles. It lives in the intestines and helps prevent intestinal infections. Taking antibiotics can disturb the body's balance of friendly bacteria, which is why eating yogurt when taking antibiotics is frequently recommended.

Chilled Creations

Because it's best if some smoothie ingredients are chilled while others are frozen, dairy products are a natural in smoothies as they fall into both categories and provide nutrients not found in fruits. Here are some dairy options you can use in your smoothies:

◆ **Milk.** Chances are you've got a quart of some sort of milk in the refrigerator. But if you haven't had a glass of milk since kindergarten, you might want to buy a few shelf-stable aseptic boxes of liquid milk to keep on hand for smoothies; chill them before making a smoothie Another option is powdered milk that is mixed with chilled water. Whatever type of milk you buy—from full-fat whole milk to skinny skim milk—will work in a smoothie. All milk is a good source of protein, vitamin D, calcium, riboflavin, and magnesium. All the recipes in this book have been nutritionally analyzed using 2 percent milk, which is on the lean side, unless noted otherwise.

◆ **Yogurt.** Yogurt is produced when milk is "invaded" by a friendly bacteria that causes it to coagulate and have a slightly astringent, tangy taste. Like milk, yogurt comes in a variety of nutritional profiles, including regular, low-fat, and nonfat. Except for the recipes in Chapter 6, which were calculated using nonfat yogurt, all the nutritional analysis for recipes containing yogurt were based on the use of 1 percent, low-fat yogurt. Flavored yogurts are specified in many recipes, but plain yogurt can always be substituted. You might want to increase the amount of a flavoring ingredient to compensate. Yogurt is also full of B vitamins, protein, and calcium.

◆ **Kefir.** Kefir is yogurt by another name. It's made the same way but with different beneficial bacteria as well as beneficial yeasts. The curd size is smaller than that of yogurt, which makes it easier to digest as well.

Smooth Sailing

If you want a yogurt-based smoothie to have a thicker texture, turn your yogurt into "yogurt cheese." Pour a container of yogurt (any flavor or plain) into a fine-meshed sieve set over a mixing bowl. Place the whole thing into the refrigerator for a few hours; the liquid in the yogurt will gradually separate from the solids and fall through the mesh into the bowl. When the yogurt in the sieve has reduced in volume by half (and the other half is the liquid in the bowl), discard the liquid. The remaining yogurt in the sieve will have a firmer texture, similar to silken tofu. Use this yogurt cheese if you like your smoothie thicker.

◆ **Flavored pudding.** Those little cups of shelf-stable or refrigerated puddings add a creamy texture, additional calcium, and delicious flavor to any smoothie. Some are fat free, although none of the prepared puddings are sugar free. To control sugar as well, prepare sugar-free instant pudding according to package directions, and use it in place of the prepared pudding cups specified in the recipes.

Frozen Favorites

If the fruit you're using is chilled or at room temperature, you can create a thick, creamy smoothie by using one of the following as your frozen ingredient:

◆ **Ice cream.** Ice cream is a treat just by itself, and it creates incredibly delicious smoothies. There's no question about it. The introduction of low-fat ice creams to the market has reduced the guilt over eating ice cream, and some manufacturers are now creating ice creams that are low in carbohydrates, too. Like milk, ice cream is a good source of vitamin D, calcium, and other minerals.

◆ **Frozen yogurt.** In some parts of the country, frozen yogurt is as popular as ice cream, with frozen yogurt chains proffering countless flavors—most generally lower in fat than even low-fat ice cream. You can substitute frozen yogurt for ice cream in any smoothie recipe.

Blender Beware

One health concern about frozen yogurt: Freezing yogurt kills all the beneficial bacteria present in refrigerated yogurt. The taste and texture of frozen yogurt are similar to soft ice cream, and the frozen variety usually contains less fat, but if you're after the benefits of acidophilus from yogurt, use fresh yogurt and add another frozen ingredient such as frozen fruit or ice cubes to the smoothie. Also, be aware that the tangy flavor of fresh yogurt is usually masked by flavor additions in the frozen product; some say this is an improvement, while others prefer a little tanginess. It's up to you.

◆ **Sorbet and sherbet.** *Sorbet* is the French word for "sherbet"; it's *grainta* in Italian. Although both are most often fruit-flavored ices, the difference between how we use sorbet and sherbet is that sorbet is not made with any dairy product. It is just fruit and water churned to a smooth consistency.

The Joy of Soy

No wonder they call it a wonder food! Lately, researchers are discovering more and more nutritional benefits from soy products. For example, soybeans are the only known plant source of *complete protein*. In addition, the Food and Drug Administration (FDA) has approved a health claim stating that diets containing 25 grams of soy protein a day may reduce the risk of heart disease.

Ellen on Edibles _____

Complete protein is the term used for a food that contains all the essential amino acids in the appropriate proportions that are part of the growth and maintenance of cells. Meats and some dairy products have complete protein, while grains and beans contain incomplete proteins. Blending incomplete proteins such as rice and beans produces complete protein. But in the plant world, soy alone has it all.

In addition, soy is low fat, and products made from soy create great smoothies. Here are a few:

◆ **Soy milk.** This nondairy "milk" is made by grinding soybeans to a flourlike consistency, cooking the flour with water, and pressing out the liquid. Soy milk is rich in protein and iron, and most manufacturers fortify their soy milk with calcium as well. It's available in many flavors (I like chocolate) as well as plain. There are also whole and low-fat versions. Soy milk can be used interchangeably with dairy milk in any smoothie recipe.

◆ **Silken tofu.** Tofu is a curd made from pressed and drained soybeans and comes in a number of densities, such as firm and silken, depending on how hard it was pressed during manufacture. Tofu is high in B vitamins, potassium, and iron, and some tofu is also high in calcium, if that mineral was

Blender Beware _____

Although you can use firm tofu to make a smoothie, do not substitute tempeh for tofu. Tempeh is made from fermented soybeans, and its crumbly texture and savory flavor are not really compatible with many fruits.

used as the curdling agent. The best tofu for smoothies is silken tofu, because it adds a soft texture to the drink. If you're using a firmer tofu, you might want to add additional liquid to the blender.

◆ **Frozen tofu.** Tofutti is the best-known brand of frozen tofu, but now many others are appearing on the market. Use frozen tofu in place of frozen yogurt or ice cream to make smoothies. It comes in a variety of flavors and has the same fat-free profile as other soy-based products.

Other Beneficial Binders

In a smoothie, it's the binder's job to make the drink creamy. Some fruits such as bananas serve this purpose, as do the dairy and soy products listed in this chapter. If you want a few other options, here you go:

◆ **Coconut milk.** Coconut milk is not the liquid that spurts out when you whack open a coconut. It's a canned concoction that results from mixing boiling water with grated coconut meat and straining out the solids to produce a "milk." Coconut milk gives smoothies a creamy texture and a delicious and decidedly coconut flavor. Don't confuse it with sweetened cream of coconut, which is used for making some drinks. Unfortunately, coconut milk is high in both calories and fat, although the fat is healthful omega-6 fatty acid. There's now a light coconut milk on the market, and that's what the recipes in this book call for.

◆ **Almond milk.** Although not a true milk, almond milk tastes like milk and has a slightly sweet almond flavor. It's made by grinding almonds with water and, usually, a sweetener. Commercial brands have the consistency of skim milk. As in other nuts, the fat in almonds is a "friendly" monounsaturated fat. It is also rich in vitamin E and has a high calcium content.

Smooth Sailing _____

You can make a rich almond milk easily by combining 2 cups blanched almonds, 2½ cups water, and ¼ cup honey or maple syrup in a blender. Blend until smooth, and refrigerate the almond milk for up to a week or freeze it in ice cube trays for up to 6 months. You can buy blanched almonds in supermarkets, or blanch them yourself. Soak the shelled almonds in boiling water for 5 minutes, drain them in a colander, and then rub off the skins between your fingers. Decreasing the water produces a thicker almond milk, while increasing it produces a thinner flavor and texture.

◆ **Peanut butter.** Peanuts are not actually nuts. They're legumes, and they're a good source of protein, vitamin E, vitamin B$_1$, niacin, and iron. Buy all-natural peanut butters if you want the best. Although you might have to stir them (the oil and solids tend to separate), they do not contain *hydrogenated oils*. Peanut butter is specified in many recipes for its flavor, and you can add a few tablespoons to any smoothie if you want a distinctive peanut taste.

Ellen on Edibles _____

Hydrogenated oils are polyunsaturated vegetable oils that have been chemically transformed from their liquid state to a hard state by the addition of additional hydrogen atoms. Once hydrogenated, the fats are saturated, and contain trans fatty acids.

◆ **Sesame paste (tahini).** Tahini is a paste made from ground sesame seeds. You can find it in most supermarkets and Middle Eastern markets. An excellent source of calcium and vitamin E, it gives smoothies a creamy texture with a slightly nutty, sesame flavor. Use it in place of peanut butter if you're not a peanut fan or if you have an allergy to peanut products.

Powerful Powders

You can easily turn a smoothie into an energy- and nutrient-packed meal. Just add a few tablespoons of a nutritional supplement for additional protein, vitamins, and minerals. You should be able to find most of the supplements listed here in many grocery and most health food stores.

I include these supplements in some of the recipes in Chapters 9 and 10, but feel free to experiment and add them whenever you want an additional boost from your beverage.

- **Bee pollen.** Bee pollen is made from the seeds of flower blossoms that stick to the bees' legs as they're going about their tasks. When they return to their hive, they clean their legs, mixing these seeds with nectar and their own enzymes to form the pollen. It's rich with protein; vitamins A, B, C, and E; as well as calcium and magnesium. Bee pollen doesn't change the taste of smoothies at all, so add up to 2 tablespoons to any smoothie recipe.

- **Carob.** Made from the ground pods of a Mediterranean evergreen, carob is very rich in calcium. Because it is similar in color and flavor to chocolate, plus it doesn't have the caffeine of chocolate and has very little fat, it has long been popular with nutrition-conscious people. Feel free to substitute carob powder tablespoon for tablespoon for chocolate in these recipes. It is naturally sweet, so no additional sugar is required. You can also add a few tablespoons to any recipe you think might benefit from the taste of chocolate.

- **Flaxseed.** Flaxseed is the best vegetable source for essential omega-3 fatty acids, the same beneficial fat found in salmon and other fish. Flaxseed also contains lecithin, which aids in digestion. The seeds have to be ground up to release their benefits, so put up to 2 tablespoons into any smoothie recipe and blend away. Flaxseed does have a nutty flavor, but it will probably be masked by other ingredients in the smoothie.

- **Soy protein powder.** There are protein powders on the market made from cow's milk or eggs, but the most popular is a flavorless powder with all the health benefits of soybeans. The texture of some brands tends to be a bit grainy, but you can add 2 or 3 tablespoons per smoothie recipe and the texture from the other ingredients will mask that of the powder.

♦ **Wheat germ.** Wheat germ is the embryo of a wheat berry, and adding just 1 tablespoon to a smoothie recipe adds 2 grams protein and 1 gram fiber. Wheat germ has a slightly nutty flavor, but that will be masked by the fruit and creamy ingredients in smoothies. Wheat germ is an exceptional source of vitamin E and also contains thiamin and copper. Add up to 2 tablespoons per recipe—or more if you like the nutty flavor.

Smooth Sailing

It's best to add all nutritional supplements to smoothies at the beginning of the blending process. Ones such as flaxseed and wheat germ benefit from being puréed well as other ingredients are added to the blender.

Great Garnishes

You might think it's crazy to garnish a smoothie. After all, you've already got a food with a luscious texture and (most of the time) a vivid color.

But there are those occasions when you might have a few extra minutes and want to make the smoothie more special. Or maybe it's a special occasion and you want to elicit a "Wow!" when you serve the drinks.

Whatever your reason, garnish away! Because smoothies are so thick, you can float almost anything on top without worrying that it'll sink in.

Ingredient Oriented

Adding any of these garnishes adds textural diversity to your smoothie experience:

♦ **Fruit kebabs.** This is the no-brainer of garnishes. Reserve some of the fruit used in the smoothie and thread bite-size pieces onto a toothpick or a little plastic sword that doubles as a toothpick. For a fancier look, use a few different types of fruit.

◆ **Strawberry "fans."** Reserve the large strawberries from your box for the garnish before you purée the rest. Rinse the berries, but do not remove the green cap. Using a sharp paring knife, make five or six cuts through the berry, starting at the cap. Transfer the strawberry to a plate, and gently push apart the slices to form a fan.

◆ **Cookies.** Here's another no-brainer. Any sort of crisp cookie, especially little rolled pirouettes, are great to stick in the top of a smoothie.

◆ **Chocolate shavings.** Any smoothie that contains chocolate will benefit from chocolate shavings. Use the large holes of a box grater to grate a chocolate bar, and then sprinkle the shavings over the top of the smoothie.

◆ **Chocolate leaves.** Brush a thick layer of melted chocolate on the underside of well-washed heavy leaves of a nontoxic plant, such as lemon or holly. Chill, then pull away the leaf and the chocolate will have molded into a veined pattern.

Smooth Sailing

Chocolate can absorb aromas and flavors from other foods, so always wrap it tightly after it's been opened. Store chocolate in a cool, dry place, but do not refrigerate or freeze it. If chocolate is stored at a high temperature, the fat will rise to the surface and become a whitish powder called a bloom. It will disappear, however, as soon as the chocolate is melted.

◆ **Chocolate-dipped fruit.** Chop white or dark chocolate finely, and melt it in a double boiler over simmering water or in the microwave. Microwave on medium (50 percent) power for 30-second intervals, stirring the chocolate as it melts. Fairly dry fruits are the best for dipping. Use strawberries (rinsed and patted dry on paper towels) or large dried fruit such as dried apricots or dried pineapple. Dip the fruit in the melted chocolate, and then place it on a sheet of plastic wrap until the chocolate has set.

◆ **Herb sprigs.** These fall into the "maybe they'll eat them or maybe they won't" category, but a sprig of fresh, bright green mint adds color along with its fresh aroma to any fruit smoothie. Rinse the sprigs, and tuck one upright along the side of the smoothie glass.

◆ **Sprinkle of cinnamon.** Cinnamon is a wonderful complement to many fresh fruit flavors. Just give a sprinkle on the top.

◆ **Crispy tortilla triangles.** Cut a 6-inch flour tortilla into 8 wedges. Brush the triangles with melted butter and sprinkle them with cinnamon sugar. Bake on a baking sheet in a 400°F oven for 5 minutes or until crisp. Cool the triangles to room temperature, and place a few into the top of the smoothie.

◆ **Cheese crisps.** These are great stuck into the top of any on-the-savory-side vegetable smoothies. Preheat the oven to 375°F. Place 1-tablespoon mounds of grated cheddar cheese 3 inches apart on an un-greased baking sheet. Bake the cheese for 5 to 7 minutes or until melted and brown around the edges. Remove the baking sheet from the oven, and allow the crisps to cool. Remove them gently with a spatula.

Blender Beware

You can place fresh fruit on the top of a smoothie in advance, but add any crisp garnish as the smoothies are on the way to the table so you don't end up with soggy garnish.

Lovely to Look At

The garnishes in the previous section can be popped into your mouth while you're drinking the smoothie. This group, however, is meant for looks only:

◆ **Pineapple foliage.** If you cut up a fresh pineapple for a smoothie, pull out a few leaves from the green crown, rinse them, and stick them in the drink.

◆ **Orange knots.** Peel an orange, and cut the peel into very thin strips. Tie one in a knot, then loop another one through the knot and tie it, too. Vary the look by using some orange rind with some lemon rind.

◆ **Paper umbrellas.** You can find these at many party stores and gourmet shops, and people love the looks of the brightly colored umbrellas sticking out of the top of a smoothie.

The Least You Need to Know

◆ Yogurt contains a beneficial bacteria that helps promote intestinal health.

◆ Tahini can be used in place of peanut butter in recipes to add a sesame rather than peanut flavor, and to avoid a potential peanut allergy.

◆ You can add a number of flavorless nutritional supplements to your smoothies to increase their nutritional content.

◆ Carob is a powder that tastes similar to chocolate but does not contain caffeine.

◆ For special occasions or to just dress up your smoothies, garnish them with edible or nonedible flourishes.

Fantastic Fruits (and Veggies) for Every Diet

Fruits, from creamy bananas to bowls of berries, are synonymous with smoothies in many people's minds. In Part 2, you learn how you can best use these nutritious foods to create meals in a glass.

The recipes all contain fruit (and in the last chapter some veggies and herbs are included, too). You'll find smoothies made with calcium-rich dairy products, protein-rich soy foods, foods low in fat, and foods relatively low in carbohydrates.

Part of the fun of these recipes is that they can be personalized to suit your tastes. Any smoothie made with cow's milk can also be made with soy milk, and vice versa. If you're counting carb grams and not calories, you can exchange whole milk for skim milk and have a richer treat.

4

Dairy Smoothies

In This Chapter

- ◆ Recipes with high-calcium dairy products
- ◆ Smoothies with yogurt and frozen yogurt
- ◆ Dairy and fruit smoothies

Dairy products are natural smoothie binders. By definition, dairy products are creamy, and they lend this consistency to the finished drinks. Fruit and dairy also complement each other, as dairy products contain nutrients that are primarily different from those in fruit.

Dairy products are an excellent source of protein and calcium, and even skim milk has the same amount of calcium whole milk does. The majority of the protein in milk is casein, a complete protein. Pasteurization does kill the natural vitamins A and D in dairy products, but this is added back by fortification during processing. In addition to calcium, dairy products contain minerals such as phosphorus, magnesium, and zinc.

Suffice it to say, these dairy-containing recipes are good and good for you! And the dairy products are combined with a cornucopia of luscious flavors from fruits and other ingredients.

Banana Orange Smoothie

Prep time: less than 10 minutes • Makes: 2 (15-ounce) servings

Each serving has: 199 calories • 0 calories from fat • 0 g fat • 0 g saturated fat • 7 g protein • 33 g carbohydrates

1 large banana, peeled and sliced

1 (8-oz.) container plain or banana low-fat yogurt

4 orange juice ice cubes or ½ cup orange juice

½ cup orange sorbet or sherbet

Combine banana and yogurt in a blender. Blend on high speed until banana is puréed and mixture is smooth. Add orange juice cubes and sorbet. Blend on high speed again until mixture is smooth. Serve immediately.

Variation: In place of sorbet, you can use an additional ½ cup orange juice.

Smooth Sailing

If you want to use ice in a smoothie for a frostier flavor and thicker texture but don't want to take the time to freeze juice, use this shortcut: add 1 tablespoon juice concentrate for every 2 or 3 ice cubes used.

Banana Honey Smoothie

Prep time: less than 10 minutes   •   Makes: 2 (15-ounce) servings

Each serving has: 504 calories   •   103 calories from fat   •   11½ g fat
•   7 g saturated fat   •   8½ g protein   •   94 g carbohydrates

1 (8-oz.) container low-fat vanilla
yogurt or 1 cup vanilla frozen
yogurt

½ cup vanilla-flavored coffee
creamer

⅓ cup honey

1 TB. lemon juice

2 frozen, sliced large bananas

Combine yogurt, coffee creamer,
honey, and lemon juice in a blender.
Blend on high speed until smooth.
Add bananas and blend on high speed
again until bananas are puréed and
mixture is smooth. Serve immediately.

Variations: You can use plain yogurt
and plain light cream or milk in this
recipe. If using them in place of the
vanilla-flavored products, add ¼ teaspoon pure vanilla extract.

 **Smooth Sailing**

Whipping cream
should not be frozen in liquid
form because it will separate,
but it can be frozen once it's
whipped. If you have leftover
whipped cream, freeze it in
ice cube trays and use it for
making smoothies.

Banana Mixed Fruit Smoothie

Prep time: less than 10 minutes   •   Makes: 2 (15-ounce) servings

Each serving has: 301 calories   •   9 calories from fat   •   1 g fat   •
0 g saturated fat   •   6 g protein   •   70 g carbohydrates

1 (8-oz.) container strawberry low-fat yogurt

½ cup orange juice

1 large banana, peeled and sliced

½ cup seedless red grapes

½ cup frozen strawberries

½ cup frozen peach slices

Blender Beware

There is no standard size for small yogurt containers. They range from 4 ounces to 8 ounces. If your favorite brand is less than 8 ounces, compensate by adding some additional liquid.

Combine yogurt, orange juice, banana, and grapes in a blender. Blend on high speed until banana is puréed and mixture is smooth. Add strawberries and peaches. Blend on high speed again until fruit is puréed and mixture is smooth. Serve immediately.

Variations: Use raspberries in place of strawberries, apricots instead of peaches, and peach nectar in place of orange juice.

Purely Peach Smoothie

Prep time: less than 10 minutes   •   Makes: 2 (15-ounce) servings

Each serving has: 274 calories   •   27 calories from fat   •   3 g fat   •
1 g saturated fat   •   6½ g protein   •   54 g carbohydrates

¾ cup chilled peach *nectar*

1 (8-oz.) container peach low-fat yogurt

1½ cups frozen peach slices (2 large peaches, peeled, sliced, and frozen, or presliced peaches from frozen food aisle)

½ cup vanilla frozen yogurt or vanilla ice cream

Dash almond extract (optional)

Combine peach nectar, yogurt, and peaches in a blender. Blend on high speed until peaches are puréed and mixture is smooth. Add frozen yogurt and almond extract (if using). Blend on high speed again until smooth. Serve immediately.

Variation: This smoothie can also be made with apricot nectar and fresh apricots.

Ellen on Edibles

Nectar, which comes from the Latin and Greek words meaning "drink of the gods," is just a fancy word for juice. Nectar is usually used in conjunction with tree fruits such as peaches and apricots, and it's made with a concentrated fruit purée that's mixed with some corn syrup, giving it a thicker texture than that of a citrus juice.

Peach and Raspberry Smoothie

Prep time: less than 10 minutes   •   Makes: 2 (15-ounce) servings

Each serving has: 294 calories   •   27 calories from fat   •   3 g fat   •
1 g saturated fat   •   7 g protein   •   60 g carbohydrates

1 (8-oz.) container raspberry low-fat yogurt

½ cup chilled peach nectar

¾ cup raspberries

1½ cups frozen peach slices (2 large peaches, peeled, sliced, and frozen, or presliced peaches from frozen food aisle)

½ cup vanilla frozen yogurt or vanilla ice cream

Combine yogurt, peach nectar, and raspberries in a blender. Blend on high speed until smooth. Add peaches and frozen yogurt. Blend on high speed again until fruit is puréed and mixture is smooth. Serve immediately.

Variations: Use orange juice in place of peach nectar and strawberries in place of raspberries.

Smooth Sailing

Rather than dirtying a measuring cup each time you need to measure ice cream or frozen yogurt, measure the capacity of your ice-cream scoop. Then you'll know how many scoops to add without having to use the extra measuring cup.

Ginger Peach Smoothie

Prep time: less than 10 minutes   •   Makes: 2 (15-ounce) servings

Each serving has: 264 calories   •   9 calories from fat   •   1 g fat   •
½ g saturated fat   •   7 g protein   •   59 g carbohydrates

1 cup chilled peach nectar	1½ cups frozen peach slices (2 large peaches, peeled, sliced, and frozen, or presliced peaches from frozen food aisle)
1 (8-oz.) container peach low-fat yogurt	
2 TB. *crystallized ginger*	

Combine peach nectar, yogurt, and crystallized ginger in a blender. Blend on high speed until smooth. Add peaches and blend on high speed again until peaches are puréed and mixture is smooth. Serve immediately.

Variation: Use apricot nectar or orange juice in place of peach nectar.

 Ellen on Edibles

Ginger comes in a number of different forms, ranging from fresh root in the produce section to ground ginger in the spice aisle. **Crystallized ginger** is a cross between the two. It's in the spice aisle, but its flavor is more akin to fresh than dried. It's ginger that's been candied in sugar syrup, and it's much milder than ground ginger. So if you must substitute ground ginger, use ¼ teaspoon for each tablespoon crystallized ginger called for.

Caramel Apple Smoothie

Prep time: less than 10 minutes • Makes: 2 (15-ounce) servings

Each serving has: 363 calories • 72 calories from fat • 8 g fat •
3½ g saturated fat • 6 g protein • 71 g carbohydrates

¾ cup 2 percent milk

⅓ cup caramel sauce

2 sweet eating apples, such as
McIntosh, Jonathan, or York
Imperial, peeled, cored, and diced

¾ cup vanilla frozen yogurt or
vanilla ice cream

Combine milk, caramel sauce, and apples in a blender. Blend on high speed
until apples are puréed and mixture is smooth. Add frozen yogurt and
blend on high speed again until smooth. Serve immediately.

Variations: Use soy milk in place of cow's milk in this or any smoothie
recipe. Use butterscotch sauce as an alternative to caramel sauce.

Smooth Sailing

Whether or not you want to take the time to peel the apples when
making smoothies is up to you. If you're using an apple with a red
skin, you will have bits of peel in the drink, regardless of how long you
purée it. However, the skin contains nutrients and fiber, so it's a trade-off
as to whether you want to save time and gain some nutrients or have a
smoothie that's truly smooth.

Apple Pie Smoothie

Prep time: less than 10 minutes • Makes: 2 (15-ounce) servings

Each serving has: 242 calories • 72 calories from fat • 8 g fat •
4 g saturated fat • 3 g protein • 47 g carbohydrates

½ cup chilled apple juice

½ cup chilled applesauce

1 sweet eating apple, such as
McIntosh, Jonathan, or York
Imperial, peeled, cored, and diced

½ tsp. apple pie spice or ¼ tsp.
ground cinnamon and ¼ tsp. grated
nutmeg

1 cup vanilla frozen yogurt or
vanilla ice cream

¼ cup granola (optional)

Combine apple juice, applesauce,
apple, and apple pie spice in a blender. Blend on high speed until apple
is puréed and mixture is smooth. Add
frozen yogurt and blend on high
speed again until smooth. Add granola
(if using), and pulse blender on and
off at low speed to incorporate granola,
but do not purée granola. Serve immediately.

Variations: Add ¼ cup walnuts to the
blender instead of the granola and garnish the smoothie with raisins or more
chopped nuts.

Blender Beware

If you're using a
smoothie maker rather than
a blender to make smoothies,
don't add any crunchy ingredients such as granola to the
jar, as it will clog the dispens-
ing spigot. Pour the drinks
into glasses and then stir in
the crunchy ingredient with
a spoon.

Strawberry Cheesecake Smoothie

Prep time: less than 10 minutes • Makes: 2 (15-ounce) servings

Each serving has: 398 calories • 216 calories from fat • 24 g fat • 15 g saturated fat • 10 g protein • 38 g carbohydrates

1 (8-oz.) container strawberry low-fat yogurt

⅓ cup sour cream

1 (3-oz.) pkg. cream cheese

2½ cups strawberries

3 ice cubes

Combine yogurt, sour cream, and cream cheese in a blender. Blend on high speed until mixture is smooth. Add strawberries and ice cubes, and blend on high speed again until strawberries are puréed and mixture is smooth. Serve immediately.

Smooth Sailing

If you don't have flavored yogurt, you can always substitute plain yogurt and then add 2 tablespoons fruit jam to the recipe.

Variation: You can use almost any yogurt and fruit combination for this recipe, such as peach, raspberry, blueberry, or cherry. It's best if the yogurt and fruit are the same flavor.

Blackberry Blueberry Smoothie

Prep time: less than 10 minutes • Makes: 2 (15-ounce) servings

Each serving has: 248 calories • 9 calories from fat • 1 g fat •
1 g saturated fat • 5½ g protein • 54 g carbohydrates

1 (8-oz.) container blackberry low-fat yogurt

1 cup orange juice

1 TB. lemon juice

1½ cups frozen blueberries

½ cup frozen blackberries, or additional ½ cup blueberries

Combine yogurt, orange juice, and lemon juice in a blender. Blend on high speed until mixture is smooth. Add blueberries and blackberries, and blend on high speed again until fruit is puréed and mixture is smooth. Serve immediately.

Variation: Use peach or apricot nectar in place of orange juice.

Blender Beware

When substituting fruits for one another in a smoothie recipe, keep in mind that the color of the fruit is important because fruits blend with one another when they are puréed. Before making a substitution, think about how it will look when it's blended.

Cherry Vanilla Smoothie

Prep time: less than 10 minutes • Makes: 2 (15-ounce) servings

Each serving has: 311 calories • 63 calories from fat • 7 g fat • 3 g saturated fat • 10 g protein • 56 g carbohydrates

1 (8-oz.) container vanilla low-fat yogurt

¾ cup 2 percent milk

1 TB. lemon juice

1½ cups frozen sweet pitted cherries

½ cup vanilla frozen yogurt or vanilla ice cream

Combine yogurt, milk, and lemon juice in a blender. Blend on high speed until mixture is smooth. Add cherries and frozen yogurt, and blend on high speed again until fruit is puréed and mixture is smooth. Serve immediately.

Variation: You can use strawberries, peaches, or blueberries in place of cherries.

Smooth Sailing

The lemon or lime juice added to smoothie recipes does not make them tart because the juice is added in such a small quantity. Instead, the tart citrus juice accentuates the vibrant flavor of the fruits.

Double Apricot Smoothie

Prep time: less than 10 minutes • Makes: 2 (15-ounce) servings

Each serving has: 303 calories • 63 calories from fat • 7 g fat •
3 g saturated fat • 6 g protein • 56 g carbohydrates

1 cup chilled apricot nectar

½ cup 2 percent milk

1½ cups sliced apricots

10 dried apricot halves, *unsulfured* if possible

¾ cup vanilla frozen yogurt

Combine apricot nectar, milk, apricot slices, and dried apricots in a blender. Blend on high speed until fruit is puréed and mixture is smooth. Add frozen yogurt and blend on high speed again until smooth. Serve immediately.

Variation: This can become a Double Peach Smoothie if you substitute peach nectar, peach slices, and 4 dried peaches.

Ellen on Edibles

Unsulfered dried fruits have not been sprayed with sulfur dioxide, a gas used for fumigation that destroys the fruit's B vitamins. Most health food stores are good sources for naturally dried fruits.

Pineapple Coconut Smoothie

Prep time: less than 10 minutes   •   Makes: 2 (15-ounce) servings

Each serving has: 406 calories   •   234 calories from fat   •   26 g fat   •
25 g saturated fat   •   6 g protein   •   37 g carbohydrates

1 cup canned light coconut milk

1 (8-oz.) container peach low-fat yogurt

1 TB. lime juice

1½ cups frozen pineapple cubes

Combine coconut milk, yogurt, and lime juice in a blender. Blend on high speed until mixture is smooth. Add pineapple and blend on high speed again until pineapple is puréed and mixture is smooth. Serve immediately.

Variation: Substitute coconut sorbet for coconut milk; then use chilled pineapple rather than frozen.

Smooth Sailing

When devising a recipe, part of the process is selecting secondary ingredients that enhance the primary flavors. In this case, the peach yogurt adds a pink glow as well as its delicate flavor to balance the coconut and pineapple.

Mango Pineapple Smoothie

Prep time: less than 10 minutes   •   Makes: 2 (15-ounce) servings

Each serving has: 256 calories   •   9 calories from fat   •   1 g fat   •
1 g saturated fat   •   6 g protein   •   56 g carbohydrates

1 (8-oz.) container peach low-fat yogurt

½ cup orange juice

1 cup diced mango

1 cup diced pineapple

½ cup frozen banana slices

Combine yogurt, orange juice, mango, and pineapple in a blender. Blend on high speed until mango is puréed and mixture is smooth. Add banana slices and blend on high speed again until smooth. Serve immediately.

Variation: Substitute cubes of papaya for mango, and peach nectar in place of orange juice.

 Smooth Sailing

If you're using canned pineapple rather than fresh, always buy pineapple packed in juice rather than sugar syrup. You can then use the juice in the recipe in place of the orange juice.

Mango Strawberry Smoothie

Prep time: less than 10 minutes • Makes: 2 (15-ounce) servings

Each serving has: 244 calories • 20 calories from fat • 2 g fat • 1 g saturated fat • 7½ g protein • 51 g carbohydrates

1 (8-oz.) container strawberry yogurt	1 TB. lime juice
½ cup milk	1½ cups diced mango
	1 cup frozen strawberries

Combine yogurt, milk, lime juice, and mango in a blender. Blend on high speed until mango is puréed and mixture is smooth. Add strawberries and blend on high speed again until mixture is smooth. Serve immediately.

Variations: Substitute raspberry yogurt and raspberries for strawberries, and papaya for mango.

 Smooth Sailing

You can make smoothies richer or less rich depending on the dairy product you select. Choose skim milk for a less-rich smoothie or, at the other end of the spectrum, choose heavy cream for a richer drink.

Creamy Prune Smoothie

Prep time: less than 10 minutes   •   Makes: 2 (15-ounce) servings

Each serving has: 314 calories   •   20 calories from fat   •   2½ g fat   •
1 g saturated fat   •   9 g protein   •   68 g carbohydrates

1 (8-oz.) container vanilla low-fat yogurt

½ cup 2 percent milk

¾ cup pitted prunes

1 fresh plum, rinsed, stone removed, and sliced

4 ice cubes

Combine yogurt, milk, prunes, and plum in a blender. Blend on high speed until fruit is puréed and mixture is smooth. Add ice cubes and blend on high speed again until smooth. Serve immediately.

Variation: Substitute orange juice cubes or ½ cup vanilla frozen yogurt for plain ice.

Blender Beware

Most dried fruits today, especially prunes, are very soft. But if your fruit has dried out, soften it a little by covering it with very hot tap water for 10 minutes and then draining it before continuing with the recipe.

Date and Banana Smoothie

Prep time: less than 10 minutes • Makes: 2 (15-ounce) servings

Each serving has: 515 calories • 45 calories from fat • 5 g fat • 2½ g saturated fat • 9 g protein • 114 g carbohydrates

1 (8-oz.) container banana low-fat yogurt

½ cup orange juice

¾ cup pitted, chopped dates

2 bananas, peeled and sliced

½ cup vanilla frozen yogurt

Smooth Sailing

When buying dried dates, you might find some that are already chopped into small cubes and marketed as "baking dates." Use these to save time.

Combine yogurt, orange juice, dates, and bananas in a blender. Blend on high speed until fruit is puréed and mixture is smooth. Add frozen yogurt and blend on high speed again until smooth. Serve immediately.

Variation: Use chopped, dried figs in place of chopped dates.

Chapter 5

Nondairy Smoothies

In This Chapter

- ◆ Smoothies made creamy with frozen bananas
- ◆ Recipes using soy milk and silken tofu
- ◆ Drinks including tropical fruit nectars

It doesn't take cream, or any dairy product for that matter, to make a smoothie creamy, as you'll learn by the end of this chapter. Some recipes get their thick texture from the inherently creamy nature of bananas. Others use healthful soy products—the only plant food that provides complete protein.

And some smoothies in this chapter depend on the combination of luscious fruits for their flavor and consistency. For whatever reason you want to make a nondairy smoothie, you'll find delicious options here.

Banana Colada Smoothie

Prep time: less than 10 minutes • Makes: 2 (15-ounce) servings

Each serving has: 323 calories • 162 calories from fat • 18 g fat • 17 g saturated fat • 5 g protein • 36 g carbohydrates

½ cup canned light coconut milk

½ cup plain soy milk

1½ cups diced pineapple

⅓ cup lightly packed shredded coconut

1 frozen, sliced large banana

Smooth Sailing

This smoothie can do double duty as breakfast in the morning and a cocktail at night. Make some extra and add some dark rum or coconut rum to the mixture for an adult libation. (For more after-hours sippers, see Chapter 14.)

Combine coconut milk, soy milk, pineapple, and coconut in a blender. Blend on high speed until pineapple is puréed and mixture is smooth. Add banana and blend on high speed again until banana is puréed and mixture is smooth. Serve immediately.

Variation: Instead of banana, you can use 1 cup frozen mango or papaya cubes.

Triple Strawberry Smoothie

Prep time: less than 10 minutes • Makes: 2 (15-ounce) servings

Each serving has: 280 calories • 45 calories from fat • 5 g fat • 1½ g saturated fat • 6 g protein • 57 g carbohydrates

½ cup cranberry juice

½ cup strawberry soy milk

½ cup silken tofu

¼ cup strawberry jam

2 cups frozen strawberries

Combine cranberry juice, soy milk, tofu, and jam in a blender. Blend on high speed until mixture is smooth. Add strawberries and blend on high speed again until fruit is puréed and mixture is smooth. Serve immediately.

Variations: If you can't find strawberry soy milk or only have plain, add 2 tablespoons strawberry jam. You can substitute raspberries or blueberries for the strawberries.

Blender Beware

Tofu is very perishable, so you should always use it within a few days of opening it. To prolong its refrigerated life up to a week, drain the water from around the tofu as soon as you open the package. Refill the package with fresh water, then change the water daily, and wrap it tightly with plastic wrap.

Banana Apricot Coconut Smoothie

Prep time: less than 10 minutes • Makes: 2 (15-ounce) servings

Each serving has: 377 calories • 117 calories from fat • 13 g fat • 12 g saturated fat • 2 g protein • 43 g carbohydrates

1 cup chilled apricot nectar	¼ cup shredded coconut
¾ cup canned light coconut milk	1 frozen, sliced large banana
3 fresh apricots, diced	

Combine apricot nectar, coconut milk, apricots, and coconut in a blender. Blend on high speed until fruit is puréed and mixture is smooth. Add banana and blend on high speed again until banana is puréed and mixture is smooth. Serve immediately.

Variation: Use peach nectar and 2 fresh peaches in place of apricot nectar and apricots.

 Smooth Sailing

Even bright green bananas will ripen if left on the counter for 3 or 4 days, but you can speed up the process by placing them in a paper bag with an apple or two. The apples release a gas that causes bananas to ripen faster.

Almond Peach Smoothie

Prep time: less than 10 minutes • Makes: 2 (15-ounce) servings

Each serving has: 330 calories • 81 calories from fat • 9 g fat • 1 g saturated fat • 9 g protein • 51 g carbohydrates

1 (8-oz.) container peach nonfat yogurt

¾ cup chilled peach nectar

½ tsp. pure almond *extract*

¼ cup blanched almonds

1½ cups frozen peach slices (2 large peaches, peeled, sliced, and frozen, or presliced peaches from frozen food aisle)

Combine yogurt, peach nectar, almond extract, and almonds in a blender. Blend on high speed until nuts are puréed and mixture is smooth. Add peaches and blend on high speed again until smooth. Serve immediately.

Variation: Use apricot nectar and 3 apricots in place of peach nectar and peaches.

Ellen on Edibles

Extract is a substance with a highly concentrated flavor from evaporation or distillation. It adds a powerful flavor to foods without changing the volume or texture since you add just a small amount.

Banana Nut Smoothie

Prep time: less than 10 minutes • Makes: 2 (15-ounce) servings

Each serving has: 404 calories • 202 calories from fat • 22½ g fat
• 1 g saturated fat • 16 g protein • 40 g carbohydrates

¾ cup plain soy milk

½ cup silken tofu

½ cup chopped walnuts, toasted in
a 350°F oven for 5 minutes

½ tsp. ground cinnamon

Pinch of ground nutmeg

2 frozen, sliced large bananas

Ellen on Edibles

A **pinch** of herbs or
spices means just that. It's
the amount you can pick up
between your thumb and
index finger. It is far less than
even ¼ teaspoon.

Combine soy milk, tofu, walnuts,
cinnamon, and nutmeg in a blender.
Blend on high speed until nuts are
puréed and mixture is smooth. Add
bananas and blend on high speed
again until bananas are puréed and
mixture is smooth. Serve immediately.

Variation: Substitute pecans or
almonds for walnuts.

Banana Blueberry Smoothie

Prep time: less than 10 minutes • Makes: 2 (15-ounce) servings

Each serving has: 301 calories • 18 calories from fat • 2 g fat •
1 g saturated fat • 7 g protein • 65 g carbohydrates

1 cup plain soy milk

¼ cup blueberry jam

1½ cups blueberries

1 frozen, sliced large banana

Combine soy milk, jam, and blueberries in a blender. Blend on high speed
until blueberries are puréed and mixture is smooth. Add banana and blend
on high speed again until fruit is
puréed and mixture is smooth. Serve
immediately.

Variation: Substitute strawberry or
raspberry jam and the corresponding
fruit for blueberry jam and blueberries.

Blender Beware

Fruits such as blueber-
ries, strawberries, and raspberries can stain counters as
well as clothing. To prevent
getting messy juice all over,
after washing berries, drain
them in a colander set on a
plate.

Plum, Peach, and Banana Smoothie

Prep time: less than 10 minutes • Makes: 2 (15-ounce) servings

Each serving has: 228 calories • 31 calories from fat • 3½ g fat • 1 g saturated fat • 7 g protein • 44 g carbohydrates

½ cup plain soy milk

½ cup chilled peach nectar

½ cup silken tofu

½ tsp. pure vanilla extract

2 plums, pitted and diced

1 large peach, peeled, pitted, and sliced, or ¾ cup frozen peach slices

1 frozen, sliced large banana

Combine soy milk, peach nectar, tofu, vanilla, and plums in a blender. Blend on high speed until plums are puréed and mixture is smooth. Add peach and banana, and blend on high speed again until fruit is puréed and mixture is smooth. Serve immediately.

Variation: Use apricot nectar and 3 apricots instead of peach nectar and peaches.

Smooth Sailing

Many recipes in this chapter list both soy milk and silken tofu as ingredients, but these soy products can be used interchangeably. However, substituting all soy milk for tofu will create a smoothie with a slightly thinner texture.

Cranberry Orange Smoothie

Prep time: less than 10 minutes • Makes: 2 (15-ounce) servings

Each serving has: 237 calories • 0 calories from fat • 0 g fat • 0 g saturated fat • 1 g protein • 60 g carbohydrates

½ cup cranberry juice

¼ cup cranberry sauce

2 navel oranges, peeled, pith removed, and diced

½ cup orange sorbet

4 orange juice ice cubes or ½ cup orange juice

Combine cranberry juice, cranberry sauce, and oranges in a blender. Blend on high speed until oranges are puréed and mixture is smooth. Add sorbet and orange juice, and blend on high speed again until mixture is smooth. Serve immediately.

Variation: Substitute peaches, peach sorbet, and ice cubes made from peach nectar for orange flavors.

Smooth Sailing

If you have a metal ice-cream scoop, run it under hot tap water before trying to scoop sorbet or ice cream. This will make the frozen foods much easier to scoop.

Pineapple Mango Smoothie

Prep time: less than 10 minutes • Makes: 2 (15-ounce) servings

Each serving has: 280 calories • 36 calories from fat • 4 g fat • 1 g saturated fat • 9 g protein • 53 g carbohydrates

¾ cup plain soy milk

½ cup silken tofu

2 cups diced pineapple

1 cup mango sorbet

Combine soy milk, tofu, and pineapple in a blender. Blend on high speed until pineapple is puréed and mixture is smooth. Add sorbet and blend on high speed again until mixture is smooth. Serve immediately.

Variation: Use lemon, lime, passion fruit, or raspberry sorbet instead of mango sorbet.

Blender Beware

Canned pineapple does not deliver the same aromatic richness as fresh, but it can be substituted successfully in smoothie recipes. Do be sure that the canned fruit is packed in natural juice rather than heavy syrup. The syrup is just sugar water and adds empty calories.

Passion Fruit Smoothie

Prep time: less than 10 minutes   •   Makes: 2 (15-ounce) servings

Each serving has: 248 calories   •   36 calories from fat   •   4 g fat   •
1 g saturated fat   •   7 g protein   •   76 g carbohydrates

¾ cup silken tofu   2 cups diced pineapple

½ cup chilled passion fruit juice   ¾ cup passion fruit sorbet

Combine tofu, passion fruit juice, and pineapple in a blender. Blend on
high speed until pineapple is puréed and mixture is smooth. Add sorbet
and blend on high speed again until mixture is smooth. Serve immediately.

Variation: Use mango, both as a juice and as a sorbet, instead of passion
fruit.

Smooth Sailing

> In many supermarkets, tropical juices such as passion fruit, guava,
> mango, and papaya are stocked with the Hispanic foods rather
> than with the other juices. Such national brands as Goya produce a
> large variety of tropical fruit juices and nectars.

Strawberry Mango Smoothie

Prep time: less than 10 minutes   •   Makes: 2 (15-ounce) servings

Each serving has: 190 calories   •   22 calories from fat   •   2½ g fat   •
1 g saturated fat   •   5 g protein   •   41 g carbohydrates

¾ cup *guava* nectar

½ cup silken tofu

1½ cups strawberries

½ cup diced mango

1 frozen, sliced small banana

Ellen on Edibles

Guava is an incredibly sweet and fragrant fruit from South America and Hawaii. It is rarely available except where it's grown, but guava juice is sold in many markets, and retains high quantities of vitamins A and C.

Combine guava nectar, tofu, strawberries, and mango in a blender. Blend on high speed until fruit is puréed and mixture is smooth. Add banana and blend on high speed again until banana is puréed and mixture is smooth. Serve immediately.

Variations: Substitute apricot or peach nectar for guava nectar, and raspberries for strawberries.

Pear and Apricot Smoothie

Prep time: less than 10 minutes • Makes: 2 (15-ounce) servings

Each serving has: 255 calories • 22 calories from fat • 2½ g fat • 1 g saturated fat • 5 g protein • 55 g carbohydrates

¾ cup chilled apricot nectar

½ cup silken tofu

3 small ripe pears, peeled, cored, and diced, or 1 (15-oz.) can pears, drained and diced

10 dried apricot halves, unsulfured if possible

4 ice cubes

Combine apricot nectar, tofu, pears, and dried apricots in a blender. Blend on high speed until fruit is puréed and mixture is smooth. Add ice cubes and blend again on high speed until mixture is smooth. Serve immediately.

Variation: For a totally apricot experience, substitute 3 apricots for pears.

Smooth Sailing

Like bananas, pears ripen better off the tree than on. Pears ripen from the inside out, so if the surface is soft, chances are the fruit is overly ripe. Press gently on the stem end to see if a pear is ripe, and never store a pear in a plastic bag at room temperature or in the refrigerator. Pears need fresh oxygen, or they will "breathe" internally, which causes brown spots.

Peach and Papaya Smoothie

Prep time: less than 10 minutes • Makes: 2 (15-ounce) servings

Each serving has: 252 calories • 36 calories from fat • 4 g fat • 1½ g saturated fat • 7 g protein • 51 g carbohydrates

¾ cup chilled peach nectar

1 cup diced papaya

2 large peaches, peeled, pitted, and sliced

Smooth Sailing

Any churned frozen dessert, such as frozen tofu, frozen yogurt, or ice cream, has air beaten into the mixture. If you're substituting silken tofu for frozen tofu, use ¼ cup less.

1 cup vanilla frozen tofu or ¾ cup silken tofu and ½ tsp. pure vanilla extract

Combine peach nectar, papaya, and peaches in a blender. Blend on high speed until fruit is puréed and mixture is smooth. Add frozen tofu and blend on high speed again until mixture is smooth. Serve immediately.

Variation: Substitute mango for papaya in this recipe.

Orange Date Smoothie

Prep time: less than 10 minutes   •   Makes: 2 (15-ounce) servings

Each serving has: 458 calories   •   0 calories from fat   •   0 g fat   •
0 g saturated fat   •   1 g protein   •   115 g carbohydrates

1 cup orange juice	2 navel oranges, peeled, pith
1 TB. lemon juice	removed, and diced
1 cup chopped dates	½ cup orange sorbet

Combine orange juice, lemon juice, dates, and oranges in a blender. Blend on high speed until dates are puréed and mixture is smooth. Add sorbet and blend on high speed again until mixture is smooth. Serve immediately.

Variation: Use dried figs or raisins in place of chopped dates.

Blender Beware

Softening sorbets and other frozen treats in the microwave will make for easy scooping, but keep in mind that the smaller the quantity, the less time you should microwave it. A full half-gallon would be safe at 20 to 30 seconds, but a partially used pint should only be softened for 8 to 10 seconds.

Maple Date Nut Smoothie

Prep time: less than 10 minutes • Makes: 2 (15-ounce) servings

Each serving has: 591 calories • 198 calories from fat • 22 g fat • 2 g saturated fat • 16 g protein • 96 g carbohydrates

½ cup plain soy milk

3 TB. pure maple syrup

1 large sweet eating apple, such as McIntosh, Jonathan, or York Imperial, peeled, cored, and diced

½ cup chopped walnuts

¾ cup chopped dates

½ cup vanilla frozen tofu

Blender Beware

Note that this and other recipes in this book list "pure maple syrup" as the ingredient. Artificially flavored pancake syrup is a poor substitute.

Combine soy milk, maple syrup, apple, walnuts, and dates in a blender. Blend on high speed until mixture is puréed and smooth. Add frozen tofu and blend on high speed again until mixture is smooth. Serve immediately.

Variation: Substitute pecans or almonds for walnuts.

Raisin Bran Smoothie

Prep time: less than 10 minutes • Makes: 2 (15-ounce) servings

Each serving has: 375 calories • 36 calories from fat • 4 g fat •
1½ g saturated fat • 10 g protein • 74 g carbohydrates

¾ cup plain soy milk

¼ tsp. ground cinnamon

2 cups seedless red grapes

½ cup dark raisins

½ cup vanilla frozen tofu

¼ cup granola

Combine soy milk, cinnamon, grapes, and raisins in a blender. Blend on high speed until fruit is puréed and mixture is smooth. Add frozen tofu and blend on high speed again until mixture is smooth. Add granola and pulse on and off a few times to distribute cereal. Serve immediately.

Variation: Use seedless green grapes and golden raisins instead of red grapes and dark raisins.

Smooth Sailing

They're small in size, but dried fruits such as raisins or dates take a long time to purée in the blender. Wait until you don't see large particles remaining before you turn off the blender.

6

Low-Fat Smoothies

In This Chapter

◆ Smoothies made with nonfat dairy products

◆ Drinks made from just a variety of fruits

◆ Recipes for smoothies made with fat-free sorbets

Low fat (or no fat) can be high flavor, as you will find when making the recipes in this chapter. This becomes increasingly important as the nutritional community continues to conclude that, except in extreme moderation, there is really no such thing as "good fat" in our diets. Although saturated fat has been known as a health culprit for years, even moderate quantities of other fats can contribute to high cholesterol and heart disease.

Many grocery store shelves are stocked with fat-free dairy products. They provide all the protein and calcium those with fat do, and the thick purée of fruits in the smoothies made with these fat-free or low-fat goodies disguise their thinner mouth feel.

Also in this chapter are some recipes made from fruits alone. In many cases, the thick smoothie texture comes from the inclusion of vividly flavored fat-free fruit sorbets.

So if you're watching your fat intake or just want some good-for-you, low-fat smoothies, you've come to the right place.

Mixed Citrus Smoothie

Prep time: less than 10 minutes • Makes: 2 (15-ounce) servings

Each serving has: 266 calories • 0 calories from fat • 0 g fat • 0 g saturated fat • 2 g protein • 64 g carbohydrates

1 cup orange juice

3 *clementines*, peeled, pith removed, seeded if necessary, and diced

1 grapefruit, peeled, pith removed, seeded, and diced

1 TB. lime juice

1 cup orange sorbet

Combine orange juice, clementines, grapefruit, and lime juice in a blender. Blend on high speed until fruit is puréed and mixture is smooth. Add sorbet and blend on high speed again until smooth. Serve immediately.

Variation: Substitute 2 navel oranges or 2 tangerines for clementines. Use lime or lemon sorbet instead of orange.

Ellen on Edibles

Clementines are a citrus fruit from the mandarin orange family (as are tangerines). They are smaller than most citrus, and the peel is very thin and easy to remove. They are almost always seedless, so if you're substituting a tangerine, be sure to discard any seeds.

Banana Cherry Smoothie

Prep time: less than 10 minutes   •   Makes: 2 (15-ounce) servings

Each serving has: 286 calories   •   0 calories from fat   •   0 g fat   •
0 g saturated fat   •   8 g protein   •   64 g carbohydrates

1 (8-oz.) container cherry-vanilla
nonfat yogurt

½ cup skim milk

Pinch of ground cinnamon

1 cup cherries, pitted and halved

2 frozen, sliced bananas

Combine yogurt, milk, cinnamon,
and cherries in a blender. Blend on
high speed until cherries are puréed
and mixture is smooth. Add bananas
and blend on high speed again until
bananas are puréed and mixture is
smooth. Serve immediately.

Variation: Substitute strawberry
yogurt and strawberries for cherries.

Smooth Sailing

The cinnamon in this
recipe adds a subtle boost to
the other flavors in the drink.
Such a small amount is not
detectable as a separate flavor, but it does accentuate the
fruits.

Banana Apricot Smoothie

Prep time: less than 10 minutes   •   Makes: 2 (15-ounce) servings

Each serving has: 202 calories   •   0 calories from fat   •   0 g fat   •
0 g saturated fat   •   6 g protein   •   60 g carbohydrates

½ cup chilled apricot nectar	2 apricots, pitted and diced
1 (8-oz.) container banana nonfat yogurt	8 dried apricot halves, unsulfured if possible
1 large navel orange, peeled, pith removed, seeded, and diced	1 frozen, sliced large banana

Combine apricot nectar, yogurt, orange, apricots, and dried apricots in
a blender. Blend on high speed until fruit is puréed and mixture is smooth.
Add banana and blend on high speed again until smooth. Serve immediately.

Variation: Use peach nectar, 1 large peach, and 4 dried peach halves
instead of their apricot equivalents.

> ### Smooth Sailing
>
> The white membrane that separates the citrus sections can be bitter
> if used in recipes. But if you don't want to take the time to remove
> it from the orange sections, try this method: after you cut off all the rind
> and pith, cut the orange in half lengthwise and cut out the core as you
> would a pineapple.

Papaya Banana Smoothie

Prep time: less than 10 minutes   •   Makes: 2 (15-ounce) servings

Each serving has: 233 calories   •   0 calories from fat   •   0 g fat   •
0 g saturated fat   •   6 g protein   •   48 g carbohydrates

1 (8-oz.) container vanilla nonfat yogurt

½ cup orange juice

1 TB. lime juice

1½ cups diced papaya

1 frozen, sliced large banana

Combine yogurt, orange juice, lime juice, and papaya in a blender. Blend on high speed until papaya is puréed and mixture is smooth. Add banana and blend on high speed again until smooth. Serve immediately.

Variations: Substitute mango for papaya and a tropical fruit nectar for orange juice.

 **Blender Beware**

When freezing a banana, always cut it into slices no more than ½-inch thick. Larger pieces can tax the blender's motor before the drink becomes smooth.

Mixed Berry Smoothie

Prep time: less than 10 minutes   •   Makes: 2 (15-ounce) servings

Each serving has: 275 calories   •   0 calories from fat   •   0 g fat   •
0 g saturated fat   •   6 g protein   •   63 g carbohydrates

1 (8-oz.) container strawberry non-fat yogurt

½ cup chilled apple juice

1 cup blueberries

1 cup frozen strawberries

½ cup frozen raspberries

 Smooth Sailing

The larger the pieces of frozen fruit, the longer they will take to purée. Small blueberries or raspberries will take about half the time of peach slices or strawberries.

Combine yogurt, apple juice, and blueberries in a blender. Blend on high speed until blueberries are puréed and mixture is smooth. Add strawberries and raspberries, and blend on high speed again until smooth. Serve immediately.

Variation: Use any combination of fresh and frozen berries in this recipe. Just be sure the nonfrozen fruit is puréed first.

Cantaloupe Lemon Smoothie

Prep time: less than 10 minutes   •   Makes: 2 (15-ounce) servings

Each serving has: 157 calories   •   0 calories from fat   •   0 g fat   •
0 g saturated fat   •   1 g protein   •   40 g carbohydrates

¾ cup orange juice   2 cups diced cantaloupe

2 TB. lemon juice   ½ cup lemon sorbet

Combine orange juice, lemon juice, and cantaloupe in a blender. Blend on
high speed until cantaloupe is puréed and mixture is smooth. Add sorbet
and blend on high speed again until smooth. Serve immediately.

Variations: Make this also with honeydew melon. Substitute lime juice and
lime sorbet for lemon.

Blender Beware

Cantaloupe is one of the few fruits that's been documented to
carry salmonella bacteria. To avoid any danger, wash the entire
rind with a mild soap and water and rinse it well before cutting through
the cantaloupe. This will prevent cross-contamination of bacteria from the
rind to the melon.

Cantaloupe Berry Smoothie

Prep time: less than 10 minutes • Makes: 2 (15-ounce) servings

Each serving has: 240 calories • 0 calories from fat • 0 g fat • 0 g saturated fat • 6 g protein • 55 g carbohydrates

1 (8-oz.) container strawberry nonfat yogurt

¼ cup cranberry sauce

2 cups diced cantaloupe

½ cup frozen strawberries

Combine yogurt, cranberry sauce, and cantaloupe in a blender. Blend on high speed until cantaloupe is puréed and mixture is smooth. Add strawberries and blend on high speed again until smooth. Serve immediately.

Variation: Use raspberry yogurt and frozen raspberries instead of strawberry yogurt and strawberries.

Smooth Sailing

Cantaloupes and other melons with soft skins can be diced like onions. After you remove the peel, cut the melon in half. Then cut each half into three or four horizontal slices, and cut each lengthwise in both directions.

Watermelon Cherry Smoothie

Prep time: less than 10 minutes • Makes: 2 (15-ounce) servings

Each serving has: 184 calories • 0 calories from fat • 0 g fat •
0 g saturated fat • 5 g protein • 40 g carbohydrates

1 (8-oz.) container cherry nonfat yogurt

1 TB. lemon juice

1½ cups diced seedless watermelon

¾ cup frozen, pitted cherries

Combine yogurt, lemon juice, and watermelon in a blender. Blend on high speed until watermelon is puréed and mixture is smooth. Add cherries and blend on high speed again until smooth. Serve immediately.

Variations: Substitute strawberry yogurt and strawberries or raspberry yogurt and raspberries for cherry yogurt and cherries.

Blender Beware

Seedless watermelons are easy to find in the market, but should you have the surprise of cutting one open and finding seeds, carefully remove all the seeds before blending.

Cranberry Apple Smoothie

Prep time: less than 10 minutes • Makes: 2 (15-ounce) servings

Each serving has: 244 calories • 0 calories from fat • 0 g fat •
0 g saturated fat • 1 g protein • 61 g carbohydrates

1 cup cranberry juice

¼ cup cranberry sauce

2 large sweet eating apples, such as McIntosh, Jonathan, or York Imperial, peeled, cored, and diced

4 ice cubes

Combine cranberry juice, cranberry sauce, and apples in a blender. Blend on high speed until apples are puréed and mixture is smooth. Add ice cubes and blend on high speed again until smooth. Serve immediately.

Variation: Use 2 large peaches, peeled and sliced, instead of apples.

Smooth Sailing

Because the apples are going to be puréed, you don't need to worry about how neat the slices are. A time-saving way to cut peeled apples is to hold them over the blender and cut off slices as you turn the fruit. You will soon be down to the core, which you can then discard. This method is much faster than quartering and coring the apple.

Blueberry Apple Smoothie

Prep time: less than 10 minutes • Makes: 2 (15-ounce) servings

Each serving has: 311 calories • 0 calories from fat • 0 g fat •
0 g saturated fat • 6 g protein • 73 g carbohydrates

1 cup unsweetened applesauce

1 (8-oz.) container blueberry nonfat
yogurt

¼ cup apricot jam

Pinch of ground cinnamon

1 cup frozen blueberries

Combine applesauce, yogurt, jam,
and cinnamon in a blender. Blend on
high speed until mixture is smooth.
Add blueberries and blend on high
speed again until smooth. Serve
immediately.

Variation: Use peach yogurt and
frozen peaches instead of blueberry
yogurt and blueberries.

Blender Beware

Berries of all types are
delicate and should always
be rinsed in cold water. Even
tepid water can cause the
innate nutrients to escape right
down the drain.

Spiced Apple Smoothie

Prep time: less than 10 minutes • Makes: 2 (15-ounce) servings

Each serving has: 339 calories • 0 calories from fat • 0 g fat • 0 g saturated fat • 9 g protein • 77 g carbohydrates

1 (8-oz.) container vanilla nonfat yogurt

½ cup unsweetened applesauce

⅓ cup mango *chutney*

2 large sweet eating apples, such as McIntosh, Jonathan, or York Imperial, peeled, cored, and diced

½ cup vanilla nonfat frozen yogurt

Combine yogurt, applesauce, chutney, and apples in a blender. Blend on high speed until apples are puréed and mixture is smooth. Add frozen yogurt and blend on high speed again until smooth. Serve immediately.

Variation: For a more complex flavor, use strawberry or raspberry yogurt in place of vanilla in this recipe.

Ellen on Edibles

Chutney, from the Hindi word *chatni,* is a spicy Indian condiment containing some sort of fruit or vegetable, vinegar, and spices. It's always used as an accompaniment to curried dishes, but it can also be used with many foods to add a fat-free flavor accent.

Blackberry Orange Smoothie

Prep time: less than 10 minutes • Makes: 2 (15-ounce) servings

Each serving has: 212 calories • 0 calories from fat • 0 g fat • 0 g saturated fat • 2 g protein • 53 g carbohydrates

¾ cup orange juice

1 navel orange, peeled, pith removed, and diced

1½ cups blackberries

¾ cup orange sorbet

Combine orange juice, orange, and blackberries in a blender. Blend on high speed until fruit is puréed and mixture is smooth. Add sorbet and blend on high speed again until smooth. Serve immediately.

Variation: Use blueberries, raspberries, or strawberries in place of the blackberries in this recipe.

Papaya Banana Smoothie

Prep time: less than 10 minutes • Makes: 2 (15-ounce) servings

Each serving has: 188 calories • 0 calories from fat • 0 g fat • 0 g saturated fat • 2 g protein • 48 g carbohydrates

¾ cup chilled apricot nectar

½ cup orange juice

1½ cups diced papaya

1 frozen, sliced large banana

Smooth Sailing

When cutting fruit, it's best to use a cutting board with a well around the edges to catch the juice. Then you don't lose the juice onto the counter when you're transferring the fruit to the blender jar.

Combine apricot nectar, orange juice, and papaya in a blender. Blend on high speed until fruit is puréed and mixture is smooth. Add banana and blend on high speed again until banana is puréed and mixture is smooth. Serve immediately.

Variation: Use mango instead of papaya.

Peach and Pineapple Smoothie

Prep time: less than 10 minutes • Makes: 2 (15-ounce) servings

Each serving has: 292 calories • 0 calories from fat • 0 g fat •
0 g saturated fat • 6 g protein • 64 g carbohydrates

1 (8-oz.) container peach nonfat yogurt

½ cup pineapple juice

1 cup diced pineapple

¾ cups frozen peach slices (1 large peach, peeled, sliced, and frozen, or presliced peaches from frozen food aisle)

½ cup lemon sorbet

Combine yogurt, pineapple juice, and pineapple in a blender. Blend on high speed until pineapple is puréed and mixture is smooth. Add peach and sorbet, and blend on high speed again until smooth. Serve immediately.

Variations: Substitute peach or apricot nectar for pineapple juice. You can use 3 apricots instead of 1 peach.

 Smooth Sailing

If you're using canned pineapple for this—or any smoothie recipe—you can use the juice in the can, too, as long as the pineapple was packed in natural juice and not sugar syrup.

Chapter 7

Low-Carb Smoothies

In This Chapter

- ◆ Fruit smoothies relatively low in carbohydrates
- ◆ Recipes using binders approved on low-carbohydrate diets
- ◆ Protein-packed drinks made with tofu

Millions of people count carbs as a way of life, and if you're one of them, there's no reason smoothies can't be part of your healthy living program. In addition to gaining needed fresh fruits, you can always toss some silken tofu into a smoothie to increase your protein count.

Although certain fruits, such as bananas and all dried fruits, are relatively high in carbohydrates, melons and most berries contain only a modest amount. These are the centerpieces for the recipes in this chapter.

Fruits contain the "good carbs" of the food world, so called because they are complex carbs that release their energy gradually. In addition to fruits, whole grains share the halo. These foods are contrasted with the "bad carbs" of overly refined simple carbohydrates, such as white flour, table sugar, and any baked goods that list these ingredients prominently.

It's these "bad carbs" that cause a large spike in blood sugar, followed by an immediate "down." These are the foods to avoid, and none of them have a role in these smoothies.

But even if you're not watching your carbs, you'll still love these recipes.

Watermelon Strawberry Smoothie

Prep time: less than 10 minutes   •   Makes: 2 (15-ounce) servings

Each serving has: 113 calories   •   22 calories from fat   •   2½ g fat   •
1 g saturated fat   •   4½ g protein   •   19 g carbohydrates

1½ cups diced seedless watermelon   1 TB. lemon juice

½ cup silken tofu   1 cup frozen strawberries

Combine watermelon, tofu, and
lemon juice in a blender. Blend on
high speed until fruit is puréed and
mixture is smooth. Add strawberries
and blend on high speed again until
smooth. Serve immediately.

Variations: You can use reduced-
carbohydrate strawberry yogurt in
place of tofu and substitute raspberries
for strawberries.

> **Smooth Sailing**
>
>   If you have seeds in
> the watermelon, the easiest
> way to get rid of them is to
> dice the watermelon into small
> cubes so you can find all the
> seeds easily.

Honeydew Orange Smoothie

Prep time: less than 10 minutes • Makes: 2 (15-ounce) servings

Each serving has: 155 calories • 18 calories from fat • 2 g fat • 1 g saturated fat • 3 g protein • 32 g carbohydrates

½ cup whole milk

1½ cups diced honeydew melon

2 navel oranges, peeled, pith removed, and diced

4 ice cubes

Combine milk, honeydew melon, and oranges in a blender. Blend on high speed until fruit is puréed and mixture is smooth. Add ice cubes and blend on high speed again until smooth. Serve immediately.

Variation: Substitute cantaloupe for honeydew melon.

Smooth Sailing

If you're counting carb grams, the important number is the number of net carbs. These are the ones your body actually digests after the fiber content is subtracted because fiber is not digested. On a food label, you can calculate this number by subtracting the fiber content from the total carbohydrate count.

Minted Honeydew Smoothie

Prep time: less than 10 minutes   •   Makes: 2 (15-ounce) servings

Each serving has: 267 calories   •   72 calories from fat   •   8 g fat   •
4 g saturated fat   •   9 g protein   •   39 g carbohydrates

1 cup sugar-free vanilla instant pudding, prepared according to package instructions

2 cups diced honeydew melon

¼ cup loosely packed fresh mint leaves

6 ice cubes

Combine prepared pudding, honeydew melon, and mint leaves in a blender. Blend on high speed until fruit is puréed and mixture is smooth. Add ice cubes and blend on high speed again until smooth. Serve immediately.

Variation: Use cantaloupe in place of honeydew melon.

Smooth Sailing

If you're in a rush, there's no reason to wait the 5 minutes for the instant pudding to "set up" and become thick. Just make it and add it to the blender. It will achieve its creamy texture as you're measuring the other ingredients.

Cantaloupe Strawberry Smoothie

Prep time: less than 10 minutes • Makes: 2 (15-ounce) servings

Each serving has: 170 calories • 40 calories from fat • 4½ g fat •
1 g saturated fat • 11 g protein • 21 g carbohydrates

1 (11-oz.) can low-carb strawberry
drink, such as Atkins

2 cups diced cantaloupe

1 TB. lemon juice

1 cup frozen strawberries

 Smooth Sailing

If you want to add
more protein to a smoothie,
reduce the amount of liquid
and add ½ cup silken tofu.
You'll still have fruit flavor from
the other ingredients.

Combine strawberry drink, cantaloupe, and lemon juice in a blender.
Blend on high speed until fruit is
puréed and mixture is smooth. Add
strawberries and blend on high speed
again until smooth. Serve immediately.

Variations: Substitute honeydew
melon for cantaloupe and raspberries
in place of strawberries.

Honeydew Lemon Smoothie

Prep time: less than 10 minutes • Makes: 2 (15-ounce) servings

Each serving has: 75 calories • 0 calories from fat • 0 g fat • 0 g saturated fat • 1 g protein • 19 g carbohydrates

¾ cup sugar-free lemonade

3 TB. lemon juice

2½ cups diced honeydew melon

4 ice cubes

Combine lemonade, lemon juice, and honeydew melon in a blender. Blend on high speed until fruit is puréed and mixture is smooth. Add ice cubes and blend on high speed again until smooth. Serve immediately.

Variation: Substitute cantaloupe for honeydew melon.

 Smooth Sailing

For a more intense flavor, use ice cubes made from a sugar-free fruit drink or juice. For low-carb smoothies, use any sugar-free drink.

Raspberry Watermelon Smoothie

Prep time: less than 10 minutes • Makes: 2 (15-ounce) servings

Each serving has: 112 calories • 18 calories from fat • 2 g fat • 1 g saturated fat • 6 g protein • 17 g carbohydrates

2 (4-oz.) containers reduced-carbohydrate raspberry yogurt

1½ cups diced seedless watermelon

1 TB. lemon juice

½ cup frozen raspberries

Combine yogurt, watermelon, and lemon juice in a blender. Blend on high speed until fruit is puréed and mixture is smooth. Add raspberries and blend on high speed again until smooth. Serve immediately.

Variation: Substitute strawberry yogurt and strawberries for raspberries.

Blender Beware

"Regular" yogurt is packaged in anything from 4- to 8-ounce portions, but all reduced-carb yogurts are in 4-ounce portions. Check cartons carefully to ensure you've selected the correct yogurt because there are formulation differences in reduced-carb yogurts, such as the use of artificial sweetener.

Berry Melon Smoothie

Prep time: less than 10 minutes   •   Makes: 2 (15-ounce) servings

Each serving has: 243 calories   •   36 calories from fat   •   4 g fat   •
2 g saturated fat   •   5 g protein   •   46 g carbohydrates

1 cup sugar-free vanilla instant pudding, prepared according to package directions

1½ cups diced cantaloupe

1 cup frozen seedless red grapes

½ cup frozen raspberries

Combine prepared pudding, cantaloupe, and grapes in a blender. Blend on high speed until fruit is puréed and mixture is smooth. Add raspberries and blend on high speed again until smooth. Serve immediately.

Variations: Use reduced-carb raspberry yogurt in place of pudding. Substitute honeydew melon for cantaloupe.

 Smooth Sailing

All melons contain a high percentage of water, so recipes made with melon tend to use other frozen fruits so the smoothie will have a creamy texture from the fiber content of the fruits. Melons, however, do not freeze well.

Coconut Peach Smoothie

Prep time: less than 10 minutes • Makes: 2 (15-ounce) servings

Each serving has: 267 calories • 162 calories from fat • 18 g fat •
16 g saturated fat • 4 g protein • 26 g carbohydrates

1 (13.5-oz.) can light coconut milk	1½ cups frozen peach slices (2 large peaches, peeled, sliced, and frozen, or presliced peaches from frozen food aisle)
½ cup diced fresh coconut	

Combine coconut milk and coconut in a blender. Blend on high speed until coconut is puréed and mixture is smooth. Add peaches and blend on high speed again until smooth. Serve immediately.

Variation: Substitute 1½ cups frozen diced pineapple for peaches.

Blender Beware

The carbohydrate count of regular coconut milk and light coconut milk is the same, but the fat content of regular coconut milk is much higher. You're better off with the light version.

Tangerine Grape Smoothie

Prep time: less than 10 minutes   •   Makes: 2 (15-ounce) servings

Each serving has: 204 calories   •   18 calories from fat   •   2 g fat   •
1 g saturated fat   •   5 g protein   •   44 g carbohydrates

½ cup whole milk

1 TB. lemon juice

4 clementines, peeled, pith removed, and diced

1½ cups frozen green seedless grapes

Combine milk, lemon juice, and clementines in a blender. Blend on high speed until fruit is puréed and mixture is smooth. Add grapes and blend on high speed again until smooth. Serve immediately.

Variations: Substitute 2 navel oranges for clementines. Use red seedless grapes in place of green.

 Smooth Sailing

The cream content of whole milk tends to coat the tongue and can mask other flavors. To solve this, add a small amount of lemon juice to boost the fruity flavor.

Grape and Kiwi Smoothie

Prep time: less than 10 minutes • Makes: 2 (15-ounce) servings

Each serving has: 220 calories • 18 calories from fat • 2 g fat •
1 g saturated fat • 5 g protein • 47 g carbohydrates

¾ cup sugar-free lemonade

½ cup whole milk

3 *kiwis*, peeled and diced

1½ cups frozen green seedless
grapes

Combine lemonade, milk, and kiwis in a blender. Blend on high speed until
fruit is puréed and mixture is smooth. Add grapes and blend on high speed
again until smooth. Serve immediately.

Variation: Substitute any sugar-free fruit drink for lemonade in this recipe.

Ellen on Edibles

Kiwis are small, furry ball-shaped fruits that must be peeled before
using. The green flesh dotted with black seeds is fresh and fragrant, and you know they're ripe when they can be gently pressed.

Blackberry Papaya Smoothie

Prep time: less than 10 minutes • Makes: 2 (15-ounce) servings

Each serving has: 145 calories • 18 calories from fat • 2 g fat •
1 g saturated fat • 4 g protein • 29 g carbohydrates

1 cup strawberry-orange-banana
no-calorie fruit drink, such as
Crystal Light

½ cup whole milk

1½ cups diced papaya

½ cup frozen blackberries

4 ice cubes

Combine fruit drink, milk, and
papaya in a blender. Blend on high
speed until fruit is puréed and mixture is smooth. Add blackberries
and ice cubes, and blend on high
speed again until smooth. Serve
immediately.

Variation: Use mango in place of
papaya in this recipe, or substitute
blueberries for blackberries.

Blender Beware

Refined sugar is one of
the foods highest in carbohydrates, and it takes just a little
to push you over your daily
carb limit. Check the labels of
bottled and powdered drinks
carefully because many of
them can be high in carbs.

Papaya and Citrus Smoothie

Prep time: less than 10 minutes • Makes: 2 (15-ounce) servings

Each serving has: 160 calories • 18 calories from fat • 2 g fat •
1 g saturated fat • 4 g protein • 33 g carbohydrates

½ cup sugar-free lemonade

½ cup whole milk

1 TB. lemon juice

2 navel oranges, peeled, pith removed, and diced

1 cup diced papaya

4 ice cubes

Smooth Sailing

For lighter-tasting smoothies, you can always omit the cream or dairy product and compensate with more juice. The important part is to maintain the ratio of liquids to solids.

Combine lemonade, milk, lemon juice, oranges, and papaya in a blender. Blend on high speed until fruit is puréed and mixture is smooth. Add ice cubes and blend on high speed again until smooth. Serve immediately.

Variations: Substitute mango for papaya in this recipe. Any sugar-free fruit drink can be used in place of lemonade.

Chocolate Strawberry Smoothie

Prep time: less than 10 minutes   •   Makes: 2 (15-ounce) servings

Each serving has: 152 calories   •   49 calories from fat   •   5½ g fat   •
1½ g saturated fat   •   13 g protein   •   14 g carbohydrates

1 (11-oz.) can low-carb chocolate
drink, such as Atkins

1 (4-oz.) container reduced-
carbohydrate strawberry yogurt

1½ cups frozen strawberries

Combine chocolate drink, yogurt, and strawberries in a blender. Blend on
high speed until fruit is puréed and mixture is smooth. Serve immediately.

Variations: Use reduced-carbohydrate raspberry yogurt and frozen raspberries in place of strawberries in this recipe. Or for a totally berry experience, substitute strawberry drink for chocolate.

Smooth Sailing

Low-carb drinks are formulated for a low-carb diet and are fortified
with minerals, but you can always use whole milk and mix your
own low-carb chocolate drink. Add 3 tablespoons unsweetened cocoa
powder and add artificial sweetener to taste.

Chocolate Hazelnut Smoothie

Prep time: less than 10 minutes   •   Makes: 2 (15-ounce) servings

Each serving has: 721 calories   •   585 calories from fat   •   65 g fat   •
5 g saturated fat   •   26 g protein   •   18 g carbohydrates

1 (11-oz.) can low-carb chocolate
drink, such as Atkins

1½ cups toasted hazelnuts

4 ice cubes

Combine chocolate drink, hazelnuts, and ice cubes in a blender. Blend on
high speed until nuts are puréed and mixture is smooth. Serve immediately.

Variation: Substitute toasted almonds, pecans, or walnuts for hazelnuts in
this recipe.

Smooth Sailing

To toast nuts, place them in a single layer on a baking sheet and
bake them at 350°F for 5 to 7 minutes or until lightly browned.
The toasting intensifies the nutty flavor and is worth the time.

Chapter 8

Combo Creations

In This Chapter

◆ Recipes that combine fruits and mild-tasting vegetables
◆ Smoothies that make use of your herb garden
◆ Vegetable smoothies that can double as soups

All the smoothies in this book so far have been made exclusively with fruits and no vegetables. That's about to change, though. This chapter broadens the path through the produce department to include the vegetable aisle.

In this chapter, you'll find many recipes made with carrots. Carrots and carrot juice are packed with beta-carotene, which the body converts to vitamin A. This sweet-tasting vegetable combines well with many fruits to produce smoothies with a complex flavor.

Aromatic and flavorful fresh herbs are another smoothie addition that adds complex flavor to the smoothies in this chapter. The herbs enliven the color, as well as the flavor, of the drinks.

The chapter ends with some recipes that are straight from the vegetable patch. In addition to drinking them as a healthful snack, you can serve them as a cooling summer soup. A few even include some hot pepper sauce to provide a wake-up for your taste buds.

Sweet or spicy, you'll find a garden full of smoothies here.

Carrot Citrus Smoothie

Prep time: less than 10 minutes • Makes: 2 (15-ounce) servings

Each serving has: 273 calories • 0 calories from fat • 0 g fat • 0 g saturated fat • 1 g protein • 67 g carbohydrates

¾ cup chilled carrot juice

2 carrots, trimmed, scrubbed, and sliced

3 navel oranges, peeled, pith removed, and diced

¾ cup lemon sorbet

Combine carrot juice, carrots, and oranges in a blender. Blend on high speed until carrots and oranges are puréed and mixture is smooth. Add sorbet and blend on high speed again until smooth. Serve immediately.

Variation: Substitute orange or raspberry sorbet for lemon sorbet.

Smooth Sailing

There's no need to peel carrots for this or many recipes as long as you scrub them well with a stiff brush under cold running water. Carrots are mainly peeled for aesthetic reasons, and because they are puréed in these recipes, it makes no difference if they're peeled or not.

Carrot Strawberry Smoothie

Prep time: less than 10 minutes • Makes: 2 (15-ounce) servings

Each serving has: 232 calories • 9 calories from fat • 1 g fat • 0 g saturated fat • 6 g protein • 51 g carbohydrates

1 cup chilled carrot juice

1 (8-oz.) container strawberry low-fat yogurt

2 carrots, trimmed, scrubbed, and sliced

1½ cups frozen strawberries

Combine carrot juice, yogurt, and carrots in a blender. Blend on high speed until carrots are puréed and mixture is smooth. Add strawberries and blend on high speed again until smooth. Serve immediately.

Variation: Substitute raspberry yogurt and frozen raspberries for strawberry yogurt and strawberries.

Smooth Sailing

If you have a bag of baby carrots in the refrigerator or leftovers from a crudité platter, use 6 baby carrots for every large carrot specified in a recipe. Cut them in half and give the blender an easier time.

Tomato Lemon Smoothie

Prep time: less than 10 minutes • Makes: 2 (15-ounce) servings

Each serving has: 192 calories • 0 calories from fat • 0 g fat •
0 g saturated fat • 2 g protein • 46 g carbohydrates

1 cup tomato juice

3 TB. lemon juice

4 large ripe tomatoes, cored, seeded, and diced

¼ cup lemon sorbet

Salt to taste

Combine tomato juice, lemon juice, and tomatoes in a blender. Blend on high speed until tomatoes are puréed and mixture is smooth. Add sorbet and blend on high speed again until smooth. Season with salt and serve immediately.

Variation: Substitute lime juice and lime sorbet for lemon juice and lemon sorbet.

Smooth Sailing

The easiest way to seed a tomato is to cut it in half horizontally, then, holding it over a garbage can or the sink, squeeze it gently. The seeds will pop out without losing too much juice.

Minted Grape and Cucumber Smoothie

Prep time: less than 10 minutes   •   Makes: 2 (15-ounce) servings

Each serving has: 198 calories   •   0 calories from fat   •   0 g fat   •
0 g saturated fat   •   1 g protein   •   49 g carbohydrates

1 cup chilled white grape juice

1 large cucumber, peeled, seeded, and diced

½ cup sliced celery

¼ cup lightly packed fresh mint leaves

1½ cups frozen seedless green grapes

Salt to taste

Blender Beware

Peeling an apple is optional, but peeling a cucumber is not. Most supermarket cucumbers have been coated with wax to prolong their freshness. Discard the cucumber seeds, too, as they do not purée well.

Combine grape juice, cucumber, celery, and mint leaves in a blender. Blend on high speed until vegetables are puréed and mixture is smooth. Add grapes and blend on high speed again until smooth. Season with salt and serve immediately.

Variation: Substitute purple grape juice and seedless red grapes for white grape juice and green grapes.

Beet and Strawberry Smoothie

Prep time: less than 10 minutes • Makes: 2 (15-ounce) servings

Each serving has: 207 calories • 0 calories from fat • 0 g fat •
0 g saturated fat • 1 g protein • 50 g carbohydrates

½ cup cranberry juice

¼ cup cranberry sauce

1 (15-oz.) can diced beets with juice reserved

1½ cups frozen strawberries

Combine cranberry juice, beets with juice, and cranberry sauce in a blender. Blend on high speed until beets are puréed and mixture is smooth. Add strawberries and blend on high speed again until smooth. Serve immediately.

Variation: Substitute raspberries for strawberries.

Smooth Sailing

It's easy to open a can of beets, but if you're using fresh beets, cook them first. To preserve the most nutrients, place well-scrubbed beets in a pouch of aluminum foil and bake, covered, at 400°F for 1 to 1½ hours, depending on size. Once cool enough to handle, peel the beets.

Banana and Pumpkin Smoothie

Prep time: less than 10 minutes • Makes: 2 (15-ounce) servings

Each serving has: 298 calories • 27 calories from fat • 3 g fat •
1 g saturated fat • 4 g protein • 64 g carbohydrates

½ cup 2 percent milk or plain soy milk

1 cup solid-packed canned pumpkin

¼ cup firmly packed dark brown sugar

½ tsp. ground cinnamon

2 large bananas, peeled and sliced

½ cup vanilla frozen yogurt

Blender Beware

It's important to use solid-packed canned pumpkin, which is just plain cooked pumpkin, rather than pumpkin pie filling in this recipe. Pumpkin pie filling is already seasoned and usually contains milk and eggs.

Combine milk, pumpkin, brown sugar, cinnamon, and bananas in a blender. Blend on high speed until bananas are puréed and mixture is smooth. Add frozen yogurt and blend on high speed again until smooth. Serve immediately.

Variations: Use apple pie spice in place of cinnamon. Substitute ice cream or frozen tofu for frozen yogurt.

Spicy Cantaloupe and Cucumber Smoothie

Prep time: less than 10 minutes • Makes: 2 (15-ounce) servings

Each serving has: 156 calories • 13 calories from fat • 1½ g fat •
½ g saturated fat • 6½ g protein • 43 g carbohydrates

1 (8-oz.) container plain low-fat yogurt	½ cup sliced celery
2 TB. white wine vinegar	¼ cup diced sweet onion, such as Bermuda or Vidalia
2 cups diced cantaloupe	Salt to taste
1 small cucumber, peeled, seeded, and diced	*Hot red pepper sauce* to taste

Combine yogurt, vinegar, cantaloupe, cucumber, celery, and onion in a blender. Blend on high speed until mixture is puréed and smooth. Season mixture with salt and hot red pepper sauce to taste and serve immediately.

Variation: Substitute honeydew melon for cantaloupe.

Ellen on Edibles _____

Hot red pepper sauce is distilled from fiery chili peppers usually blended with vinegar and salt. It's best to always use it sparingly, starting with only a few drops. You can always add more, but you can't take it out.

Gazpacho Smoothie

Prep time: less than 10 minutes • Makes: 2 (15-ounce) servings

Each serving has: 81 calories • 0 calories from fat • 0 g fat •
0 g saturated fat • 1 g protein • 20 g carbohydrates

½ cup chilled tomato juice

2 TB. balsamic vinegar

½ small cucumber, peeled, seeded, and diced

½ red bell pepper, seeds and ribs removed and diced

¼ cup diced sweet onion, such as Bermuda or Vidalia

3 TB. fresh *cilantro* leaves

1 garlic clove, peeled

2 large frozen cored, seeded, and diced ripe tomatoes

Salt to taste

Hot red pepper sauce to taste

Combine tomato juice, vinegar, cucumber, red bell pepper, onion, cilantro, and garlic in a blender. Blend on high speed until vegetables are puréed and mixture is smooth. Add tomatoes and blend on high speed again until smooth. Season mixture with salt and hot red pepper sauce to taste, and serve immediately.

Variations: Substitute mixed vegetable juice for tomato juice, and use any color bell pepper in place of red.

> **Ellen on Edibles** _____
>
> **Cilantro** is a member of the parsley family and is used in Hispanic and Asian dishes. This green, leafy herb is sometimes called Chinese coriander in markets. Don't confuse it with coriander seed, which comes from the same plant but packs a spicy punch that's too powerful for a smoothie.

Asian Tomato Carrot Smoothie

Prep time: less than 10 minutes   •   Makes: 2 (15-ounce) servings

Each serving has: 87 calories   •   0 calories from fat   •   0 g fat   •
0 g saturated fat   •   1 g protein   •   20 g carbohydrates

1 cup chilled carrot juice

2 TB. *rice vinegar*

1 TB. soy sauce

1 TB. peeled, coarsely chopped
fresh ginger

3 scallions, trimmed and sliced

3 TB. fresh cilantro leaves

1 garlic clove, peeled

2 large frozen cored, seeded, and
diced ripe tomatoes

Salt and ground black pepper to
taste

Combine carrot juice, vinegar, soy
sauce, ginger, scallions, cilantro, and
garlic in a blender. Blend on high
speed until vegetables are puréed and
mixture is smooth. Add tomatoes
and blend on high speed again until
smooth. Season mixture with salt and
black pepper and serve immediately.

Variation: Substitute chilled tomato
juice in place of carrot juice.

Ellen on Edibles

Rice vinegar is a very
mild vinegar used extensively
in Asian cooking. It is widely
available in supermarkets, but
if you can't find it, the best
substitute is cider vinegar.

Tomato and Basil Smoothie

Prep time: less than 10 minutes • Makes: 2 (15-ounce) servings

Each serving has: 84 calories • 0 calories from fat • 0 g fat • 0 g saturated fat • 1 g protein • 20 g carbohydrates

1 cup chilled tomato juice	3 large frozen cored, seeded, and diced ripe tomatoes
1 TB. lemon juice	Salt and ground black pepper to taste
1 cup loosely packed fresh basil leaves	

Combine tomato juice, lemon juice, and basil in a blender. Blend on high speed until basil is puréed and mixture is smooth. Add tomatoes and blend on high speed again until smooth. Season mixture with salt and black pepper and serve immediately.

Variation: Substitute ½ cup fresh oregano leaves for basil leaves.

> ### Blender Beware
>
> If you're using a fruit or vegetable juice packed in an aluminum can, always transfer any juice not used in the recipe into a glass jar or plastic bottle before placing it in the refrigerator. After a few days, the acid in juices can react with the metal and give the juice a "tinny" taste.

Dilled Cucumber Smoothie

Prep time: less than 10 minutes • Makes: 2 (15-ounce) servings

Each serving has: 98 calories • 13 calories from fat • 1½ g fat •
½ g saturated fat • 6½ g protein • 13 g carbohydrates

1 (8-oz.) container plain low-fat yogurt

2 large cucumbers, peeled, seeded, and diced

½ cup rinsed fresh *dill* leaves, stems discarded

Salt and ground black pepper to taste

Combine yogurt, cucumbers, and dill in a blender. Blend on high speed until mixture is puréed and smooth. Season mixture with salt and black pepper and serve immediately.

Variation: Use sour cream in place of yogurt.

Ellen on Edibles

Dill is a fresh-tasting, aromatic herb used in Scandinavian and many other European cuisines. Fresh dill is mild; dill seed, used in making pickles, is much spicier.

Herbed Potato Smoothie

Prep time: less than 10 minutes • Makes: 2 (15-ounce) servings

Each serving has: 301 calories • 144 calories from fat • 16 g fat •
12 g saturated fat • 2 g protein • 37 g carbohydrates

1 cup light cream

1 (15-oz.) can sliced potatoes, drained and chilled

½ cup lightly packed watercress leaves, rinsed well and drained

3 scallions, trimmed and sliced

2 tsp. fresh thyme leaves, or ½ tsp. dried

4 ice cubes

Salt and ground black pepper to taste

Blender Beware

It's important to discard the stems from herbs and use only the leaves. With herbs such as thyme and rosemary, the stems can be woody, and with tender herbs like cilantro and parsley, the stems can be bitter.

Combine cream, potatoes, watercress, scallions, and thyme in a blender. Blend on high speed until vegetables are puréed and mixture is smooth. Add ice cubes and blend on high speed again until smooth. Season mixture with salt and black pepper and serve immediately.

Variation: Substitute plain yogurt for light cream.

Part 3

Smoothies with a Kick

In this book, I present smoothies as food, not medicine. But smoothies can help keep you healthy. These recipes are nutritional bonuses.

It's easy to add a few tablespoons of soy protein powder to a smoothie and know your children are gaining that important nutrient for their diet. And for big kids, smoothies replace spent nutrients after a workout—and are a lot more fun to drink than a glass of water and a bunch of pills.

The recipes in the last chapter in Part 3 give you that "java jolt" you might need if your energy wanes. All the recipes use coffee or another high-in-caffeine liquid to pick you right up.

Chapter 9

Child-Pleasing Purées

In This Chapter

- ♦ Chocolate smoothies
- ♦ Fruit smoothies popular with kids
- ♦ Smoothies with dietary supplements to boost nutrition

For most parents, getting their kids to eat fruits (and vegetables) or to drink enough milk can be a challenge. But as the nutritionists tell us, fruits and veggies are loaded with vitamins, minerals, and other nutrients essential to good health—in fact, eating five portions of fruits and vegetables a day is believed to help prevent cancer and other diseases. And the calcium in dairy products is essential for developing bones So let smoothies solve the problem.

All the recipes in this chapter are made with foods child-tested for popularity. They are also written for smaller appetites, so if you're preparing one of these for a big kid (a.k.a. an adult), you might want to increase the portion size.

These recipes also share a common "secret ingredient." They all include a supplement to ensure that the young drinkers are receiving a healthful meal. These supplements, which enhance the nutritional profile, are flavorless, so the additional protein is your little secret.

Chocolate Banana Smoothie

Prep time: less than 10 minutes • Makes: 2 (8-ounce) servings

Each serving has: 280 calories • 27 calories from fat • 3 g fat • 1 g saturated fat • 16 g protein • 48 g carbohydrates

1 cup 2 percent chocolate milk

3 TB. chocolate syrup

2 TB. plain soy protein powder

1 frozen, sliced large banana

Smooth Sailing

If you are using regular cow's milk or soy milk in a recipe in place of chocolate milk, increase the amount of chocolate syrup by 1 tablespoon per ½ cup milk.

Combine chocolate milk, chocolate syrup, and protein powder in a blender. Blend on high speed until mixture is smooth. Add banana and blend on high speed again until smooth. Serve immediately.

Variation: Substitute plain milk and 3 tablespoons honey for chocolate milk and chocolate syrup.

Cherry Banana Smoothie

Prep time: less than 10 minutes • Makes: 2 (8-ounce) servings

Each serving has: 196 calories • 22 calories from fat • 2½ g fat • 1 g saturated fat • 5 g protein • 46 g carbohydrates

½ cup 2 percent milk

1 (4-oz.) container cherry low-fat yogurt

2 TB. cherry preserves

¾ cup cherries, pitted

2 TB. bee pollen

1 frozen, sliced large banana

Combine milk, yogurt, preserves, cherries, and bee pollen in a blender. Blend on high speed until cherries are puréed and mixture is smooth. Add banana and blend on high speed again until smooth. Serve immediately.

Variation: Substitute strawberry yogurt, strawberry preserves, and strawberries (or raspberry yogurt, raspberry preserves, and raspberries) for cherry yogurt, cherry preserves, and cherries.

 Smooth Sailing

You can substitute soy milk for cow's milk in any smoothie recipe, especially if you want to increase the protein in your children's diets or if they are lactose-intolerant.

Caramel Banana Smoothie

Prep time: less than 10 minutes • Makes: 2 (8-ounce) servings

Each serving has: 282 calories • 14 calories from fat • 1½ g fat • 1 g saturated fat • 15 g protein • 54 g carbohydrates

¾ cup 2 percent milk

⅓ cup *caramel* sauce

¼ tsp. pure vanilla extract

2 TB. plain soy protein powder

1 frozen, sliced large banana

Combine milk, caramel sauce, vanilla extract, and protein powder in a blender. Blend on high speed until mixture is smooth. Add banana and blend on high speed again until smooth. Serve immediately.

Variation: Substitute butterscotch or strawberry sauce for caramel sauce.

Ellen on Edibles

Caramel is the liquid that results when granulated sugar has been cooked to a deep golden brown, to about 350°F on a candy thermometer. Although when cooled the caramel is hard and brittle, you get a thick sauce when you add butter and cream to the browned sugar.

Peanut Butter Strawberry Smoothie

Prep time: less than 10 minutes • Makes: 2 (8-ounce) servings

Each serving has: 453 calories • 145 calories from fat • 16 g fat •
4 g saturated fat • 15 g protein • 63 g carbohydrates

½ cup 2 percent milk

1 (4-oz.) container strawberry low-fat yogurt

¼ cup smooth *peanut butter*

3 TB. strawberry preserves

2 TB. bee pollen

1 frozen, sliced large banana

Combine milk, yogurt, peanut butter, preserves, and bee pollen in a
blender. Blend on high speed until mixture is smooth. Add banana and
again blend on high speed until smooth. Serve immediately.

Variation: Substitute raspberry or cherry yogurt and the same flavor of
preserves for strawberry.

Ellen on Edibles

Peanut butter is the spread made from grinding peanuts, which
are actually legumes, not nuts. Peanuts are rich in iron and protein;
peanut butter developed as a health food in the beginning of the twenti-
eth century. You can easily make your own at home by grinding roasted
peanuts with a little peanut oil in a food processor.

Peanut Butter Banana Smoothie

Prep time: less than 10 minutes • Makes: 2 (8-ounce) servings

Each serving has: 356 calories • 342 calories from fat • 38 g fat •
9½ g saturated fat • 24 g protein • 28 g carbohydrates

1 cup 2 percent milk

¼ cup smooth peanut butter

2 TB. plain soy protein powder

1 frozen, sliced large banana

Combine milk, peanut butter, and protein powder in a blender. Blend on
high speed until mixture is smooth. Add banana and blend on high speed
again until smooth. Serve immediately.

Variation: Substitute almond butter or tahini for peanut butter.

Blender Beware

Use smooth peanut butter rather than chunky when making smoothies. The small peanut pieces in chunky peanut butter are extremely difficult to grind into a smooth drink.

Chocolate Cherry Banana Smoothie

Prep time: less than 10 minutes • Makes: 2 (8-ounce) servings

Each serving has: 330 calories • 22 calories from fat • 2½ g fat • 1 g saturated fat • 10 g protein • 65 g carbohydrates

⅔ cup 2 percent chocolate milk

1 (4-oz.) container cherry low-fat yogurt

3 TB. chocolate syrup

2 TB. bee pollen

½ cup cherries, pitted

1 frozen, sliced large banana

Combine chocolate milk, yogurt, chocolate syrup, bee pollen, and cherries in a blender. Blend on high speed until cherries are puréed and mixture is smooth. Add banana and blend on high speed until smooth. Serve immediately.

Variation: Substitute strawberry yogurt and strawberries or raspberry yogurt and raspberries for cherry yogurt and cherries.

> **Blender Beware**
> Do not substitute cocoa powder for chocolate syrup. The powder is unsweetened, and because it requires liquid for hydration, it will make a smoothie overly thick as well as bitter.

Applesauce Smoothie

Prep time: less than 10 minutes • Makes: 2 (8-ounce) servings

Each serving has: 180 calories • 18 calories from fat • 2 g fat • ½ g saturated fat • 13 g protein • 39 g carbohydrates

¾ cup unsweetened applesauce

1 (4-oz.) container vanilla pudding or ½ cup vanilla yogurt or vanilla frozen yogurt

2 TB. plain soy protein powder

¼ tsp. pure vanilla extract

1 sweet eating apple, such as McIntosh, Jonathan, or York Imperial, peeled, cored, diced, and frozen

Combine applesauce, pudding, protein powder, and vanilla extract in a blender. Blend on high speed until mixture is smooth. Add apple and blend on high speed again until smooth. Serve immediately.

Variation: Substitute butterscotch or chocolate pudding for vanilla pudding.

Smooth Sailing

Cut apple pieces turn brown if they're exposed to air for very long. If you're not using cut apple pieces right away, toss them with a solution of 1 cup water and 2 tablespoons lemon juice to prevent discoloration.

Apple Banana Smoothie

Prep time: less than 10 minutes • Makes: 2 (8-ounce) servings

Each serving has: 233 calories • 0 calories from fat • 0 g fat •
0 g saturated fat • 13 g protein • 47 g carbohydrates

¾ cup chilled apple juice

⅓ cup applesauce

1 sweet eating apple, such as
McIntosh, Jonathan, or York
Imperial, peeled, cored, and diced

2 TB. plain soy protein powder

1 frozen, sliced large banana

Combine apple juice, applesauce,
apple, and protein powder in a
blender. Blend on high speed until
apple is puréed and mixture is
smooth. Add banana and blend on
high speed until smooth. Serve immediately.

Variation: Substitute approximately
1 cup frozen strawberries for
banana.

Smooth Sailing

Substitute natural
apple cider for pasteurized
apple juice in this or any
smoothie recipe. If you're
using fresh cider, use it within
a few weeks of purchase
before it begins to ferment.

Fruit Cup Smoothie

Prep time: less than 10 minutes • Makes: 2 (8-ounce) servings

Each serving has: 177 calories • 9 calories from fat • 1 g fat • 0 g saturated fat • 14 g protein • 28 g carbohydrates

¾ cup chilled apple juice

1 (4-oz.) container peach low-fat yogurt

2 TB. plain soy protein powder

½ cup frozen strawberries

½ cup frozen blueberries

Blender Beware

You can purchase frozen strawberries at the supermarket that are whole and large and reasonably ripe. It's better, however, to freeze them yourself when they are in season. That way, you can cut them into slices before freezing, which makes them easier to blend.

Combine apple juice, yogurt, and protein powder in a blender. Blend on high speed until mixture is smooth. Add strawberries and blueberries, and blend on high speed again until smooth. Serve immediately.

Variation: Any fruit-flavored yogurt works well in this recipe, and you can substitute raspberries or any mixture of frozen berries for strawberries and blueberries.

Creamy Orange Smoothie

Prep time: less than 10 minutes • Makes: 2 (8-ounce) servings

Each serving has: 282 calories • 22 calories from fat • 2½ g fat •
1 g saturated fat • 16 g protein • 50 g carbohydrates

¾ cup orange juice

1 (4-oz.) container vanilla low-fat yogurt

2 navel oranges, peeled, pith removed, and diced

2 TB. plain soy protein powder

½ cup vanilla frozen yogurt

Combine orange juice, yogurt, oranges, and protein powder in a blender. Blend on high speed until oranges are puréed and mixture is smooth. Add frozen yogurt and blend on high speed again until smooth. Serve immediately.

Variation: Add ½ cup shredded coconut to this recipe, or substitute plain yogurt for vanilla.

 Smooth Sailing

If you want to make this or any other smoothie thicker, increase the proportion of frozen ingredients. In this recipe, freezing some of the orange juice into ice cubes will increase the thickness of the finished drink.

Purple Grape Smoothie

Prep time: less than 10 minutes • Makes: 2 (8-ounce) servings

Each serving has: 222 calories • 9 calories from fat • 1 g fat •
½ g saturated fat • 14 g protein • 41 g carbohydrates

¾ cup chilled purple grape juice

1 (4-oz.) container raspberry low-fat yogurt

2 TB. plain soy protein powder

1 cup frozen seedless red grapes

Combine grape juice, yogurt, and protein powder in a blender. Blend on high speed until mixture is smooth. Add grapes and blend on high speed again until smooth. Serve immediately.

Variation: Substitute white grape juice and green grapes for the purple grape juice and red grapes.

Smooth Sailing

If you want to freeze grapes and don't want to take the extra step of removing them from the stems and freezing them on a baking sheet, just rinse the grapes and freeze them right on the stems. The stems keep the grapes from sticking together, and they are easy to pull free even when frozen.

Grape and Blueberry Smoothie

Prep time: less than 10 minutes   •   Makes: 2 (8-ounce) servings

Each serving has: 208 calories   •   22 calories from fat   •   2½ g fat   •
1 g saturated fat   •   10 g protein   •   48 g carbohydrates

¾ cup chilled purple grape juice   ¾ cup blueberries

½ cup silken tofu   ¾ cup frozen red seedless grapes

2 TB. bee pollen

Combine grape juice, tofu, bee pollen, and blueberries in a blender. Blend
on high speed until blueberries are puréed and mixture is smooth. Add
grapes and blend on high speed until smooth. Serve immediately.

Variation: Substitute white grape juice and green grapes for purple grape
juice and red grapes.

Smooth Sailing

You might have heard that drinking red wine has heart-healthy benefits. Red grapes and red grape juice also contain the phytochemi-
cal resveratrol, which is credited with helping the heart and possibly
fighting cancer.

Grape and Banana Smoothie

Prep time: less than 10 minutes   •   Makes: 2 (8-ounce) servings

Each serving has: 238 calories   •   22 calories from fat   •   2½ g fat   •
1 g saturated fat   •   10 g protein   •   56 g carbohydrates

¾ cup chilled white grape juice

½ cup silken tofu

2 TB. bee pollen

¾ cup green seedless grapes

1 frozen, sliced large banana

Smooth Sailing

If you're using large grapes, it's best to cut them in half before adding them to the blender because large grapes can be difficult to grind into a smooth drink.

Combine grape juice, tofu, bee pollen, and grapes in a blender. Blend on high speed until grapes are puréed and mixture is smooth. Add banana and blend on high speed again until smooth. Serve immediately.

Variation: Substitute purple grape juice and red seedless grapes for white grape juice and green grapes.

Chapter 10

Power Purées

In This Chapter

- Vitamin- and mineral-replenishing smoothies
- Protein-rich smoothies
- Potassium-rich banana smoothies

When you're working out, it's important to always remain hydrated and replace fluids on a regular basis. Smoothies can do that for you. Not only do these cold drinks offer refreshment and hydration, but they also contain a number of nutrients you need after you've been working your body.

All recipes in this chapter are formulated for replenishing vitamins and minerals and are also full of flavor. Many contain nuts or nut butters that offer additional protein, and others are made creamy with bananas, a fruit high in the potassium you lose during exercise.

As with fresh fruit juices, your body can easily break down and quickly assimilate the nutrients in smoothies. Plus, these smoothies have an additional punch, thanks to the protein powders and other nutritional supplements disguised in their luscious flavors and textures.

Strawberry Cashew Smoothie

Prep time: less than 10 minutes • Makes: 2 (15-ounce) servings

Each serving has: 588 calories • 324 calories from fat • 36 g fat •
7 g saturated fat • 30 g protein • 45 g carbohydrates

1 (8-oz.) container strawberry low-
fat yogurt

½ cup silken tofu

1 cup raw *cashews*

2 TB. plain soy protein powder

1½ cups frozen strawberries

Combine yogurt, tofu, cashews, and protein powder in a blender. Blend on
high speed until cashews are puréed and mixture is smooth. Add strawberries and blend on high speed again until smooth. Serve immediately.

Variation: Substitute raspberry yogurt and frozen raspberries for strawberry yogurt and strawberries.

Ellen on Edibles

Cashews are kidney-shaped nuts that add creamy richness to
smoothies without animal fat, although they are high in both calories and polyunsaturated fat. They are also very high in magnesium,
which plays a vital role in converting carbohydrates to energy. The pods
cashews come from are toxic, so handle with care. (Most cashews are
sold shelled, however.)

Banana Sesame Smoothie

Prep time: less than 10 minutes • Makes: 2 (15-ounce) servings

Each serving has: 594 calories • 218 calories from fat • 24½ g fat • 3 g saturated fat • 29½ g protein • 75 g carbohydrates

1 cup plain soy milk	2 TB. plain soy protein powder
½ cup silken tofu	½ tsp. pure vanilla extract
⅓ cup tahini	2 frozen, sliced large bananas
3 TB. honey	

Combine soy milk, tofu, tahini, honey, protein powder, and vanilla extract in a blender. Blend on high speed until mixture is smooth. Add bananas and blend on high speed again until smooth. Serve immediately.

Variation: Substitute peanut butter for tahini. Omit honey if you're using peanut butter that contains sweeteners.

Ellen on Edibles

Tahini is a paste made from ground sesame seeds. An excellent source of calcium and vitamin E, tahini can be found in most supermarkets and Middle Eastern markets. Depending on the brand, tahini is sold in either cans or jars. Regardless, it's always important to stir it well before measuring because the oil rises to the top. Properly stirred tahini should be very thick.

Banana Raspberry Smoothie

Prep time: less than 10 minutes • Makes: 2 (15-ounce) servings

Each serving has: 395 calories • 53 calories from fat • 6 g fat • 1 g saturated fat • 26 g protein • 65 g carbohydrates

1 (8-oz.) container raspberry low-fat yogurt

¾ cup plain soy milk

½ cup silken tofu

2 TB. plain soy protein powder

1 cup raspberries

2 frozen, sliced large bananas

Smooth Sailing

If you're avoiding refined sugars, use plain yogurt in this or any other smoothie recipe. Incorporate 3 tablespoons of a fruit-only preserve for each 8-ounce container of yogurt.

Combine yogurt, soy milk, tofu, protein powder, and raspberries in a blender. Blend on high speed until raspberries are puréed and mixture is smooth. Add bananas and blend on high speed until smooth. Serve immediately.

Variation: Substitute strawberry yogurt and strawberries or blueberry yogurt and blueberries for raspberry yogurt and raspberries.

Banana Date Smoothie

Prep time: less than 10 minutes • Makes: 2 (15-ounce) servings

Each serving has: 577 calories • 54 calories from fat • 6 g fat •
1 g saturated fat • 18 g protein • 120 g carbohydrates

1 (8-oz.) container vanilla low-fat yogurt

1 cup plain soy milk

½ cup silken tofu

1 cup firmly packed pitted dates, preferably unsulfured

2 frozen, sliced large bananas

Combine yogurt, soy milk, tofu, and dates in a blender. Blend on high speed until dates are puréed and mixture is smooth. Add bananas and blend on high speed again until smooth. Serve immediately.

Variation: Substitute dried apricots or dried figs, unsulfured if possible, for dates.

 Smooth Sailing

Dates are a good source of potassium, calcium, and iron, all of which are essential nutrients after exercise. Buy natural dates not packed in sugar or corn syrup. They're sweet enough as it is!

Apple, Banana, and Peanut Butter Smoothie

Prep time: less than 10 minutes • Makes: 2 (15-ounce) servings

Each serving has: 653 calories • 315 calories from fat • 35 g fat • 7 g saturated fat • 26 g protein • 72 g carbohydrates

1 cup chilled apple juice

½ cup silken tofu

3 TB. bee pollen

½ cup smooth peanut butter

½ tsp. pure vanilla extract

2 sweet eating apples, such as McIntosh, Jonathan, or York Imperial, peeled, cored, and diced

1 frozen, sliced large banana

Blender Beware

These smoothie recipes were developed using commercial peanut butter. If you're using natural peanut butter made without sugar, add 1 to 3 tablespoons honey to the recipe.

Combine apple juice, tofu, bee pollen, peanut butter, vanilla extract, and apples in a blender. Blend on high speed until apples are puréed and mixture is smooth. Add banana and blend on high speed again until smooth. Serve immediately.

Variation: Substitute tahini for peanut butter.

Apple Blueberry Smoothie

Prep time: less than 10 minutes   •   Makes: 2 (15-ounce) servings

Each serving has: 273 calories   •   45 calories from fat   •   5 g fat   •
1 g saturated fat   •   8 g protein   •   51 g carbohydrates

2 TB. flaxseed

1 (8-oz.) container blueberry
low-fat yogurt

½ cup chilled apple juice

1 sweet eating apple, such as
McIntosh, Jonathan, or York
Imperial, peeled, cored, and diced

1 cup frozen blueberries

Blend flaxseed in a blender on high speed until seeds are pulverized. Add
yogurt, apple juice, and apple, and blend on high speed until apple is
puréed and mixture is smooth. Add blueberries and blend on high speed
again until smooth. Serve immediately.

Variation: Substitute strawberry yogurt and frozen strawberries or raspberry yogurt and frozen raspberries for blueberry yogurt and blueberries.

Ellen on Edibles

Flaxseed is the best vegetable source for essential omega-3 fatty
acids, and it also contains lecithin, which aids in digestion. You
can find flaxseed already ground, but it's best to buy it whole so it will
remain fresher longer. Note that it gets ground in the blender first, before
any other ingredients, so its hard shell will be pulverized.

Pineapple and Banana Smoothie

Prep time: less than 10 minutes • Makes: 2 (15-ounce) servings

Each serving has: 291 calories • 49 calories from fat • 5½ g fat • 1 g saturated fat • 21 g protein • 45 g carbohydrates

1 cup chilled pineapple juice

1 cup silken tofu

2 TB. lime juice

2 TB. plain soy protein powder

1 cup diced pineapple

1 large frozen, sliced banana

Smooth Sailing

Pineapples are an excellent source of bromelain, an enzyme that helps fight inflammation as well as indigestion. Pineapple is also a natural diuretic, which can be useful if you're retaining water.

Combine pineapple juice, tofu, lime juice, protein powder, and pineapple in a blender. Blend on high speed until pineapple is puréed and mixture is smooth. Add banana and blend on high speed again until smooth. Serve immediately.

Variation: Substitute apricot nectar and diced apricots for pineapple juice and pineapple.

Pineapple Ginger Smoothie

Prep time: less than 10 minutes • Makes: 2 (15-ounce) servings

Each serving has: 314 calories • 27 calories from fat • 3 g fat • ½ g saturated fat • 17 g protein • 44 g carbohydrates

1 cup chilled pineapple juice

½ cup silken tofu

¼ cup crystallized ginger

1 TB. diced *fresh ginger*

2 TB. plain soy protein powder

1½ cups frozen diced pineapple

Combine pineapple juice, tofu, crystallized ginger, fresh ginger, and protein powder in a blender. Blend on high speed until mixture is smooth. Add pineapple and blend on high speed again until smooth. Serve immediately.

Variation: Substitute mango nectar and frozen diced mango or papaya nectar and frozen diced papaya for pineapple juice and pineapple.

Ellen on Edibles

Ginger is a tropical root that should be peeled before it is sliced or diced. It is one of the best known sources of zinc of any food, has been shown to lower cholesterol, and has anti-inflammatory properties.

Mango Tahini Smoothie

Prep time: less than 10 minutes • Makes: 2 (15-ounce) servings

Each serving has: 488 calories • 193 calories from fat • 21½ g fat • 3 g saturated fat • 16½ g protein • 62 g carbohydrates

1 cup chilled mango nectar

½ cup silken tofu

⅓ cup tahini

2 TB. bee pollen

2 cups frozen diced mango

Combine mango nectar, tofu, tahini, and bee pollen in a blender. Blend on high speed until mixture is smooth. Add mango and blend on high speed again until smooth. Serve immediately.

Variation: Substitute papaya nectar and frozen diced papaya for mango nectar and mango.

Blender Beware

There are few fruits as luscious as a ripe mango—and few fruits as lip-pursing awful as a rock-hard one. If all you can find is an unripe, green mango, you're better off using papaya or jarred mango. Green mangoes will ripen faster in a paper bag with some apples.

Date and Cashew Smoothie

Prep time: less than 10 minutes • Makes: 2 (15-ounce) servings

Each serving has: 760 calories • 310 calories from fat • 34½ g fat
• 6½ g saturated fat • 117 g protein • 110 g carbohydrates

1½ cups chilled unsweetened apple-sauce

½ cup silken tofu

1 cup unsalted roasted cashews

½ tsp. ground cinnamon

1 cup firmly packed pitted dates, preferably unsulfured

4 ice cubes

Combine applesauce, tofu, cashews, cinnamon, and dates in a blender. Blend on high speed until mixture is smooth. Add ice cubes and blend on high speed again until smooth. Serve immediately.

Variation: Substitute dried figs or dried apricots, unsulfured if possible, for dates.

Smooth Sailing

Most whole food stores sell nuts in bulk, with the price depending on the size of the pieces. For smoothies, always select the least expensive (and, therefore, smallest-size) nuts you can find because you are just going to grind them up.

Almond Honey Banana Smoothie

Prep time: less than 10 minutes • Makes: 2 (15-ounce) servings

Each serving has: 804 calories • 369 calories from fat • 41 g fat •
4 g saturated fat • 32 g protein • 90 g carbohydrates

1 cup plain soy milk	¼ cup honey
1 (8-oz.) container vanilla low-fat yogurt	2 TB. plain soy protein powder
½ cup almond butter	½ tsp. pure vanilla extract
	1 large frozen, sliced banana

Combine soy milk, yogurt, almond butter, honey, protein powder, and vanilla extract in a blender. Blend on high speed until mixture is smooth. Add banana and blend on high speed again until smooth. Serve immediately.

Variation: Substitute any nut butter for almond butter.

Smooth Sailing

The color of honey is determined by the source of the flower nectar. In general, the darker the honey, the richer the flavor. Although honey is a concentrated source of sugars, it also contains amino acids, B-complex vitamins, and vitamins C, D, and E, which are not found in refined sugar.

Chapter 11

Pick-You-Up Smoothies

In This Chapter

- Caffeine-loaded smoothies
- Tea and spiced tea smoothies
- Sparkling soda smoothies

Almost everyone hits the energy wall sometime during the day. It can be first thing on those mornings you just don't want to get out of bed. For other people, the fatigue valley is mid-morning or mid-afternoon.

You can enjoy some of the smoothies in this chapter in place of your morning cup of coffee or on your drive to work—or have them any time of the day when you need a bit of a boost to replenish your energy. Many smoothies in this chapter also include ingredients with strong nutritional content as well as caffeine.

Whenever you make the smoothies in this chapter, you have the promise of a frosty, thick drink with enough caffeine to jolt you right back to feeling alert.

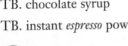

Cappuccino Smoothie

Prep time: less than 10 minutes • Makes: 2 (15-ounce) servings

Each serving has: 190 calories • 54 calories from fat • 6 g fat • 3 g saturated fat • 2 g protein • 31 g carbohydrates

1½ cups chilled strong brewed coffee

3 TB. chocolate syrup

1 TB. instant *espresso* powder

¼ tsp. ground cinnamon

4 ice cubes

¾ cup coffee frozen yogurt or ice cream

> **Ellen on Edibles**
>
> **Espresso** is a dark, strong coffee made by forcing steam through very finely ground Italian-roasted coffee beans. This liquid can then be dehydrated into an instant espresso powder similar to other instant coffee powders.

Combine coffee, chocolate syrup, espresso powder, and cinnamon in a blender. Blend on high speed until mixture is smooth. Add ice cubes and frozen yogurt, and blend on high speed again until smooth. Serve immediately.

Variation: For a more chocolate taste, substitute chocolate frozen yogurt or ice cream for coffee yogurt.

Mocha Smoothie

Prep time: less than 10 minutes   •   Makes: 2 (15-ounce) servings

Each serving has: 410 calories   •   130 calories from fat   •   14½ g fat   •   8 g saturated fat   •   3 g protein   •   64 g carbohydrates

2 cups chilled strong brewed coffee

½ cup fudge sauce

4 ice cubes

1 cup coffee frozen yogurt or ice cream

Combine coffee, fudge sauce, ice cubes, and frozen yogurt in a blender. Blend on high speed until mixture is smooth. Serve immediately.

Variation: Substitute caramel sauce for fudge sauce.

Smooth Sailing

All recipes in this chapter contain ingredients with caffeine, but if you want the taste of coffee without the "java jolt," use decaffeinated coffee. Do consider, however, that chocolate is another source of caffeine.

Banana Cappuccino Smoothie

Prep time: less than 10 minutes   •   Makes: 2 (15-ounce) servings

Each serving has: 317 calories   •   54 calories from fat   •   6 g fat   •
4 g saturated fat   •   5 g protein   •   60 g carbohydrates

1½ cups chilled strong brewed
coffee

½ cup 2 percent milk

⅓ cup chocolate syrup

¼ tsp. ground *cinnamon*

1 frozen, sliced large banana

½ cup coffee frozen yogurt or ice
cream

Combine coffee, milk, chocolate syrup, and cinnamon in a blender. Blend
on high speed until mixture is smooth. Add banana and frozen yogurt, and
blend on high speed again until smooth. Serve immediately.

Variation: Substitute chocolate or vanilla frozen yogurt or ice cream for
coffee yogurt.

Ellen on Edibles

Cinnamon is the ground inner bark of a tropical evergreen tree.
What we commonly call cinnamon is actually cassia, which has
been used since ancient times to cure colds and aid digestion. Both are
found in supermarkets, and either works well in these recipes.

Raspberry Coffee Smoothie

Prep time: less than 10 minutes   •   Makes: 2 (15-ounce) servings

Each serving has: 216 calories   •   18 calories from fat   •   2 g fat   •
1 g saturated fat   •   5½ g protein   •   42 g carbohydrates

1½ cups chilled strong brewed
coffee

1 (8-oz.) container raspberry low-fat
yogurt

1 cup frozen raspberries

¾ cup raspberry sherbet

Combine coffee, yogurt, and raspberries in a blender. Blend on high speed
until raspberries are puréed and mixture is smooth. Add sherbet and
blend on high speed again until
smooth. Serve immediately.

Variation: Substitute strawberry
yogurt, frozen strawberries, and
strawberry sorbet for raspberry
yogurt, raspberries, and raspberry
sherbet.

 Smooth Sailing

Raspberries are a
good source of vitamin C and
potassium. You must treat them
gently, though. Rinse them in
a bowl of cold water, and
then scoop them out with a
slotted spoon or your hand.
Rinsing under running water
might bruise them.

Hazelnut Espresso Smoothie

Prep time: less than 10 minutes • Makes: 2 (15-ounce) servings

Each serving has: 579 calories • 445 calories from fat • 49½ g fat
• 8½ g saturated fat • 12 g protein • 24 g carbohydrates

1½ cups chilled strong brewed
coffee

1 cup hazelnut coffee creamer

1 cup toasted *hazelnuts*

4 ice cubes

½ cup coffee frozen yogurt or ice
cream

Combine coffee, hazelnut coffee creamer, and hazelnuts in a blender. Blend
on high speed until nuts are puréed and mixture is smooth. Add ice cubes
and frozen yogurt, and blend on high speed again until smooth. Serve
immediately.

Variation: Substitute amaretto coffee creamer and toasted almonds for
hazelnut creamer and hazelnuts.

Ellen on Edibles

Hazelnuts are also called filberts, and these grape-size nuts come
primarily from the Mediterranean region. To remove the bitter skins,
roast the hazelnuts in a 350°F oven for 7 to 10 minutes. Then take a
handful and rub them between two dry dish towels. The peels will slip
right off.

Date Latte Smoothie

Prep time: less than 10 minutes • Makes: 2 (15-ounce) servings

Each serving has: 379 calories • 49 calories from fat • 5½ g fat • 3 g saturated fat • 6 g protein • 78 g carbohydrates

1½ cups chilled strong brewed coffee

1 cup pitted dates, preferably unsulfured

½ cup 2 percent milk

⅔ cup vanilla frozen yogurt or ice cream

Combine coffee, dates, and milk in a blender. Blend on high speed until dates are puréed and mixture is smooth. Add frozen yogurt and blend on high speed again until smooth. Serve immediately.

Variation: Substitute chocolate or coffee ice cream or frozen yogurt for vanilla yogurt.

Blender Beware

Be sure to cut up the dates before measuring them to ensure that all the pits have been removed. Bits of bitter date pit will never purée in a smoothie, and you will have to throw out the whole batch because smoothies are too thick to strain.

Almond Coffee Smoothie

Prep time: less than 10 minutes • Makes: 2 (15-ounce) servings

Each serving has: 443 calories • 229 calories from fat • 25½ g fat
• 13 g saturated fat • 9 g protein • 47 g carbohydrates

1½ cups chilled strong brewed coffee

½ cup almonds

1 cup crushed *amaretto* cookies

¼ tsp. pure almond extract

⅔ cup coffee frozen yogurt or ice cream

Ellen on Edibles

Amaretto is an almond-flavored liqueur made in Italy.

Combine coffee, almonds, amaretto cookies, and almond extract in a blender. Blend on high speed until nuts are puréed and mixture is smooth. Add frozen yogurt and blend on high speed again until smooth. Serve immediately.

Variation: Substitute hazelnuts, shortbread cookies, and pure vanilla extract for almonds, amaretto cookies, and almond extract.

Coffee Coconut Smoothie

Prep time: less than 10 minutes   •   Makes: 2 (15-ounce) servings

Each serving has: 500 calories   •   297 calories from fat   •   33 g fat   •
26 g saturated fat   •   6 g protein   •   49 g carbohydrates

1½ cups chilled strong brewed
coffee

1 cup shredded coconut

2 (1.61-oz.) chocolate-covered
coconut candy bar, broken into
½-inch pieces

1 cup coffee frozen yogurt or ice
cream

Combine coffee, coconut, candy bar pieces, and frozen yogurt in a blender.
Blend on high speed until mixture is smooth. Serve immediately.

Variation: Substitute chocolate frozen yogurt or ice cream for coffee
yogurt.

Smooth Sailing

The best way to brew coffee is in a French coffee press. This is a
narrow glass pitcher with a plunger that fits snugly in the pitcher
and forces the water through the coffee grounds. With the coffee
grounds in the pitcher, pour in boiling water, stir well, and let it sit for 2
minutes. Then press the plunger down over the grounds. The coffee will
be very aromatic and not bitter, and the plunger will keep the grounds
secure in the bottom of the pitcher.

Tropical Fruit Chai Smoothie

Prep time: less than 10 minutes   •   Makes: 2 (15-ounce) servings

Each serving has: 252 calories   •   36 calories from fat   •   4 g fat   •
2 g saturated fat   •   6 g protein   •   48 g carbohydrates

1½ cups chilled strong brewed *chai*

1 TB. lemon juice

¾ cup diced mango

1 cup frozen, diced pineapple

½ cup pineapple sorbet

Combine chai, lemon juice, and mango in a blender. Blend on high speed until fruit is puréed and mixture is smooth. Add pineapple and sorbet, and blend on high speed again until smooth. Serve immediately.

Variation: Substitute papaya for mango.

Ellen on Edibles

Chai is a spiced tea that originated in India. It is made with finely ground cinnamon, cardamom, cloves, pepper, and nutmeg, brewed with black tea, and then mellowed with milk.

Citrus Tea Smoothie

Prep time: less than 10 minutes • Makes: 2 (15-ounce) servings

Each serving has: 262 calories • 9 calories from fat • 1 g fat •
0 g saturated fat • 1 g protein • 63 g carbohydrates

1 cup chilled strong brewed tea

1 large grapefruit, peeled, pith removed, and diced

2 navel oranges, pith removed, peeled and diced

½ cup orange sherbet

½ cup lemon sorbet

Combine tea, grapefruit, and oranges in a blender. Blend on high speed until fruit is puréed and mixture is smooth. Add sherbet and sorbet, and blend on high speed again until smooth. Serve immediately.

Variation: Substitute 2 additional oranges for grapefruit.

Smooth Sailing

Like all citrus fruits, grapefruit is high in vitamin C, and some studies also claim the tart fruit lowers cholesterol. If you're trying to help lower your cholesterol by eating grapefruit, do not remove the white pith. That's where the cholesterol-lowering enzymes are located. But the trade-off is that the smoothies will have a bitter aftertaste from the pith.

Cherry Cola Smoothie

Prep time: less than 10 minutes • Makes: 2 (15-ounce) servings

Each serving has: 303 calories • 58 calories from fat • 6½ g fat •
4 g saturated fat • 4 g protein • 56 g carbohydrates

1 (12-oz.) chilled can *cola*

1 (4-oz.) container cherry low-fat yogurt

1 cup frozen pitted cherries

¾ cup cherry-vanilla ice cream

Combine cola, yogurt, cherries, and ice cream in a blender. Blend on high speed until fruit is puréed and mixture is smooth. Serve immediately.

Variation: Substitute strawberry yogurt, frozen strawberries, and strawberry frozen yogurt or ice cream for cherry yogurt, cherries, and cherry ice cream.

Ellen on Edibles

Cola soft drinks, which contain both caffeine and theobromine, are made from the tropical cola nut grown in Africa, South America, and the West Indies. Natives chew on the nuts themselves to fight fatigue.

Mixed Fruit Mountain Dew Smoothie

Prep time: less than 10 minutes   •   Makes: 2 (15-ounce) servings

Each serving has: 256 calories   •   9 calories from fat   •   1 g fat   •
<1 g saturated fat   •   2 g protein   •   62 g carbohydrates

1 (12-oz.) chilled can Mountain
Dew

2 navel oranges, peeled, pith
removed, and diced

1 cup frozen strawberries

½ cup raspberry sherbet

Combine Mountain Dew and oranges in a blender. Blend on high speed
until oranges are puréed and mixture is smooth. Add strawberries and
sherbet, and blend on high speed until smooth. Serve immediately.

Variation: Substitute frozen raspberries for strawberries.

Blender Beware _____

Any liquid that goes into a smoothie should be well chilled and not
at room temperature. No amount of frozen fruit will compensate for
the temperature difference, and the drink will not be frosty unless the beverage starts out that way.

Part **4**

Sweet Sensations

Call them shakes. Call them frappés. Call them malts. Whatever you call them, they're dessert smoothies, and that's what Part 4 is all about.

Some contain fresh fruit so you can pretend they're good for you—sort of like eating apple pie or strawberry shortcake. But we know that's not what it's about. It's about decadent richness.

You chocoholics will find a chapter just for you. You'll also find recipes for dessert smoothies based on popular ingredients and types of desserts. Part 4 ends with a chapter for adults only, full of dessert or after-dinner smoothies made with some sort of wine, liquor, or liqueur.

Chapter 12

Chocolate Cravings

In This Chapter

- ◆ Old-fashioned soda fountain smoothies
- ◆ Delicious chocolate smoothies
- ◆ Complex chocolate smoothies with complementary flavors

Long before there were smoothies, chocolate-loving folks were ordering malts and frappés at their local soda fountains or ice cream shops. Many of the recipes in this chapter are similar in flavor and texture to those earlier frozen drinks.

Chocolate is distinctive in itself, but it also pairs well with myriad other flavors—from ginger and mint to bananas and berries. You'll find these and other combinations in the recipes in this chapter.

But if you're not a chocolate fan, don't skip this chapter. Many of the variations tell you how to create the drinks without chocolate.

Chocolate Malted Smoothie

Prep time: less than 10 minutes • Makes: 2 (15-ounce) servings

Each serving has: 775 calories • 216 calories from fat • 24 g fat • 14 g saturated fat • 16 g protein • 134 g carbohydrates

2 cups chocolate milk

¼ cup chocolate syrup

⅓ cup *malted milk powder*

2 cups chocolate frozen yogurt or ice cream

Ellen on Edibles

Malted milk powder is made from malt, a grain that's similar to barley. Once dried, it is ground into a mellow, slightly sweet powder that's the characteristic seasoning for malts as well as malt vinegar.

Combine chocolate milk, chocolate syrup, and malted milk powder in a blender. Blend on high speed until mixture is smooth. Add frozen yogurt and blend on high speed again until smooth. Serve immediately.

Variation: For a less-intense chocolate taste, use vanilla frozen yogurt or ice cream.

Chocolate Banana Smoothie

Prep time: less than 10 minutes   •   Makes: 2 (15-ounce) servings

Each serving has: 463 calories   •   103 calories from fat   •   11½ g fat
•   6 g saturated fat   •   8 g protein   •   85 g carbohydrates

1 cup chocolate milk

¼ cup chocolate syrup

2 large bananas, peeled and sliced

1 cup chocolate frozen yogurt or ice cream

Combine chocolate milk, chocolate syrup, and bananas in a blender. Blend on high speed until bananas are puréed and mixture is smooth. Add frozen yogurt and blend on high speed again until smooth. Serve immediately.

Variation: Substitute 2 cups sliced strawberries or raspberries in place of bananas.

 Smooth Sailing

To make the Chocolate Banana Smoothie more like a banana split, garnish the glasses with chopped nuts and maraschino cherries.

Quadruple Chocolate Smoothie

Prep time: less than 10 minutes • Makes: 2 (15-ounce) servings

Each serving has: 612 calories • 234 calories from fat • 26 g fat •
15 g saturated fat • 11 g protein • 92 g carbohydrates

1½ cups chocolate milk

¼ cup chocolate syrup

½ cup semisweet chocolate chips

1 cup chocolate frozen yogurt or ice cream

Blender Beware

Although chocolate chips are small, they take a long time to completely pulverize in a blender. Allow at least 45 seconds on high speed, or you'll be chewing rather than drinking this smoothie.

Combine chocolate milk, chocolate syrup, and chocolate chips in a blender. Blend on high speed until mixture is smooth. Add chocolate frozen yogurt and blend on high speed until smooth. Serve immediately.

Variation: To create a mocha flavor, use coffee frozen yogurt or ice cream in place of chocolate yogurt.

Chocolate Walnut Smoothie

Prep time: less than 10 minutes • Makes: 2 (15-ounce) servings

Each serving has: 1,031 calories • 585 calories from fat • 65 g fat
• 11 g saturated fat • 27 g protein • 90 g carbohydrates

1½ cups chocolate milk

½ cup walnut ice cream topping

1 cup toasted walnuts

1 cup chocolate frozen yogurt or ice cream

Combine chocolate milk, walnut topping, and walnuts in a blender. Blend on high speed until walnuts are puréed and mixture is smooth. Add chocolate frozen yogurt and blend on high speed again until smooth. Serve immediately.

Variation: Substitute pecans or almonds in place of walnuts.

 Smooth Sailing

Toasting nuts enhances their flavor. Do this in advance, and freeze the nuts once toasted. The cold nuts blend easily into the smoothie and stay fresh for up to 3 months in the freezer.

Chocolate Cheesecake Smoothie

Prep time: less than 10 minutes • Makes: 2 (15-ounce) servings

Each serving has: 560 calories • 328 calories from fat • 36½ g fat • 22 g saturated fat • 13 g protein • 47 g carbohydrates

1 cup chocolate milk

1 (4-oz.) pkg. cream cheese, cut into small pieces

1 (4-oz.) container chocolate pudding

¼ cup sour cream

1 cup chocolate frozen yogurt or ice cream

 Blender Beware

Even though cream cheese is a soft cheese, it can clog up a blender if the pieces are too large. Dice all cheeses into pieces no larger than ½ inch before adding them to a blender.

Combine chocolate milk, cream cheese, chocolate pudding, and sour cream in a blender. Blend on high speed until mixture is smooth. Add chocolate frozen yogurt and blend on high speed again until smooth. Serve immediately.

Variation: Substitute plain milk, vanilla pudding, and vanilla frozen yogurt or ice cream for chocolate milk, chocolate pudding, and chocolate yogurt.

Chocolate Ginger Smoothie

Prep time: less than 10 minutes   •   Makes: 2 (15-ounce) servings

Each serving has: 476 calories   •   63 calories from fat   •   7 g fat   •
4½ g saturated fat   •   12 g protein   •   78 g carbohydrates

1½ cups chocolate milk

⅔ cup crushed gingersnap cookies

3 TB. crystallized ginger

1 cup chocolate frozen yogurt or ice cream

Combine chocolate milk, crushed cookies, and crystallized ginger in a blender. Blend on high speed until mixture is smooth. Add chocolate frozen yogurt and blend on high speed again until smooth. Serve immediately.

Variation: For a more pronounced ginger flavor, use plain milk and vanilla frozen yogurt in place of chocolate milk and chocolate yogurt.

Smooth Sailing

If you can't find crystallized ginger, use 1 tablespoon grated fresh ginger and 2 tablespoons granulated sugar instead.

Chocolate Raspberry Smoothie

Prep time: less than 10 minutes • Makes: 2 (15-ounce) servings

Each serving has: 367 calories • 63 calories from fat • 7 g fat •
3 g saturated fat • 11 g protein • 66 g carbohydrates

1 cup chocolate milk

1 (8-oz.) container raspberry low-fat
yogurt

¼ cup chocolate fudge sauce

1 cup frozen raspberries

Blender Beware

When you're buying
chocolate fudge sauce, be
sure it's not the type that hard-
ens when it's placed on top of
ice cream. This "shell," great
for a sundae, becomes gritty
in a smoothie.

Combine chocolate milk, yogurt, and
fudge sauce in a blender. Blend on
high speed until mixture is smooth.
Add raspberries and blend on high
speed again until smooth. Serve
immediately.

Variation: Substitute strawberry
yogurt and frozen strawberries
for raspberry yogurt and raspberries.

Chocolate Mint Smoothie

Prep time: less than 10 minutes   •   Makes: 2 (15-ounce) servings

Each serving has: 585 calories   •   202 calories from fat   •   22½ g fat
•   15 g saturated fat   •   12 g protein   •   93 g carbohydrates

1½ cups chocolate milk

10 small round mint candies, crushed

3 (.5-oz.) chocolate-covered peppermint candies

2 cups chocolate frozen yogurt or ice cream

Combine chocolate milk, mint candies, and peppermint candies in a blender. Blend on high speed until mixture is smooth. Add chocolate frozen yogurt and blend on high speed again until smooth. Serve immediately.

Variation: For a totally mint smoothie, use plain milk and vanilla frozen yogurt or ice cream in place of chocolate milk and chocolate yogurt.

 Smooth Sailing

The easiest way to crush hard candies is to place them in a heavy plastic bag and pound them with the bottom of a small skillet or saucepan. They'll crush in no time.

Chocolate Peanut Butter Smoothie

Prep time: less than 10 minutes • Makes: 2 (15-ounce) servings

Each serving has: 906 calories • 527 calories from fat • 58½ g fat
• 20 g saturated fat • 29 g protein • 76 g carbohydrates

1½ cups chocolate milk

4 (.8-oz.) chocolate-covered peanut butter cup candies, broken into pieces

½ cup smooth peanut butter

1½ cups chocolate frozen yogurt or ice cream

 Smooth Sailing

You can find substitutes for most candies if you think of the candy's ingredients. For example, if you don't have any peanut butter candies, add an additional ¼ cup peanut butter, 2 tablespoons sugar, and ¼ cup fudge sauce to this recipe.

Combine chocolate milk, peanut butter candy pieces, and peanut butter in a blender. Blend on high speed until mixture is smooth. Add chocolate frozen yogurt and blend on high speed again until smooth. Serve immediately.

Variation: If you want a sweet, intensely peanut taste with little chocolate, use plain milk and vanilla frozen yogurt or ice cream in place of chocolate milk and chocolate yogurt.

Caramel Chocolate Toffee Smoothie

Prep time: less than 10 minutes   •   Makes: 2 (15-ounce) servings

Each serving has: 787 calories   •   261 calories from fat   •   29 g fat   •
18 g saturated fat   •   10 g protein   •   124 g carbohydrates

1½ cups chocolate milk

½ cup caramel sauce

½ cup chocolate-covered *toffee* candies, crushed

1 cup chocolate frozen yogurt or ice cream

Combine chocolate milk, caramel sauce, and crushed toffee candies in a blender. Blend on high speed until mixture is smooth. Add chocolate frozen yogurt and blend on high speed again until smooth. Serve immediately.

Variation: For a flavor that's more caramel and less chocolate, substitute plain milk and vanilla frozen yogurt for chocolate milk and chocolate yogurt.

Ellen on Edibles

A traditional English sweet, **toffee** is similar to caramel. It's basically sugar and water boiled to a hard stage, but it's chewy because butter is added to the mixture.

Coconut Chocolate Almond Smoothie

Prep time: less than 10 minutes • Makes: 2 (15-ounce) servings

Each serving has: 908 calories • 616 calories from fat • 68 g fat •
44 g saturated fat • 12 g protein • 64 g carbohydrates

1 cup chilled canned light coconut milk

1 cup shredded coconut

½ cup toasted almonds

⅓ cup chocolate fudge sauce

1 cup chocolate frozen yogurt or ice cream

Smooth Sailing

This recipe calls for less than a can of coconut milk, so transfer the remaining milk to ice cube trays and freeze it for future use.

Combine coconut milk, coconut, almonds, and fudge sauce in a blender. Blend on high speed until mixture is smooth. Add chocolate frozen yogurt and blend on high speed again until smooth. Serve immediately.

Variation: For a coconut and almond flavor without chocolate, omit fudge sauce, increase almonds to ¾ cup, and substitute vanilla frozen yogurt for chocolate yogurt.

White Chocolate Strawberry Smoothie

Prep time: less than 10 minutes   •   Makes: 2 (15-ounce) servings

Each serving has: 640 calories   •   234 calories from fat   •   26 g fat   •
13½ g saturated fat   •   8 g protein   •   93 g carbohydrates

1 cup milk

⅔ cup *white chocolate* chips

¼ cup strawberry jam

1 cup strawberries

1 cup vanilla frozen yogurt or ice cream

Combine milk, white chocolate chips, strawberry jam, and strawberries in a blender. Blend on high speed until mixture is smooth. Add vanilla frozen yogurt and blend on high speed again until smooth. Serve immediately.

Variation: Substitute raspberry jam and raspberries for strawberry jam and strawberries.

Ellen on Edibles

White chocolate is not truly a chocolate because it doesn't contain any chocolate liquor, which is why it retains a pristine, white look. White chocolate is a combination of cocoa butter, milk solids, and sugar.

Chapter 13

Decadent Desserts

In This Chapter

- ◆ Super-rich fruit smoothies
- ◆ Nutty smoothies
- ◆ Sippable forms of your favorite desserts

Smoothies are meals in a glass. And as you'll learn from the recipes in this chapter, they're also divine desserts in a glass.

Many of these smoothies are drinkable forms of favorite desserts, like carrot cake or Key lime pie. Other recipes are made with a variety of fruits and nuts. All are rich and creamy.

Note: If you've got a chocolate craving, see Chapter 12 for a one-stop chocolate smoothie recipe chapter.

Cookies and Cream Smoothie

Prep time: less than 10 minutes • Makes: 2 (15-ounce) servings

Each serving has: 609 calories • 247 calories from fat • 27½ g fat • 12 g saturated fat • 11 g protein • 83 g carbohydrates

1 cup milk

2 cups vanilla frozen yogurt or ice cream

1 cup crushed cream-filled chocolate sandwich cookies, such as Oreo

Combine milk and vanilla frozen yogurt in a blender. Blend on high speed until mixture is smooth. Add crushed cookies and pulse on and off until cookies are finely chopped. Serve immediately.

Variation: Substitute any sort of cookie for the cream-filled chocolate sandwich cookies.

Smooth Sailing

When blending in an ingredient such as cookies, it's best to create a smooth matrix first so the cookies can retain some texture when they're added, which is why they are always added as the last ingredient.

Caramel Smoothie

Prep time: less than 10 minutes   •   Makes: 2 (15-ounce) servings

Each serving has: 582 calories   •   157 calories from fat   •   17½ g fat
•   10½ g saturated fat   •   11 g protein   •   100 g carbohydrates

1½ cups milk

½ cup caramel sauce

¼ tsp. ground cinnamon

2 cups vanilla frozen yogurt or ice cream

Combine milk, caramel sauce, and cinnamon in a blender. Blend on high speed until mixture is smooth. Add vanilla frozen yogurt and blend on high speed again until smooth. Serve immediately.

Variation: Substitute chocolate or coffee frozen yogurt for vanilla.

Blender Beware _____

Never use caramel candies in a blender because they will clog up the blades. If you don't have caramel sauce, melt caramels with milk in a microwave or in a small saucepan and then add the sauce to the blender.

Key Lime Smoothie

Prep time: less than 10 minutes • Makes: 2 (15-ounce) servings

Each serving has: 765 calories • 238 calories from fat • 26½ g fat • 16 g saturated fat • 19 g protein • 117 g carbohydrates

1 cup chilled *sweetened condensed milk*

1 cup milk

¾ cup Key lime juice

1 tsp. grated lime zest

1½ cups vanilla frozen yogurt or ice cream

Combine sweetened condensed milk, milk, lime juice, and lime zest in a blender. Blend on high speed until mixture is smooth. Add vanilla frozen yogurt and blend on high speed again until smooth. Serve immediately.

Variation: Substitute lemon juice and lemon zest for Key lime juice and lime zest.

Ellen on Edibles

Sweetened condensed milk is a canned evaporated milk that has sugar already blended into it. The mixture is simmered until about 60 percent of the liquid has evaporated before it is canned.

Strawberry Smoothie

Prep time: less than 10 minutes • Makes: 2 (15-ounce) servings

Each serving has: 374 calories • 94 calories from fat • 10½ g fat • 5½ g saturated fat • 9 g protein • 63 g carbohydrates

1½ cups milk

¼ cup strawberry jam

1 cup frozen strawberries

1 cup strawberry frozen yogurt or ice cream

Combine milk, strawberry jam, and strawberries in a blender. Blend on high speed until strawberries are puréed and mixture is smooth. Add strawberry frozen yogurt and blend on high speed again until smooth. Serve immediately.

Variation: Substitute raspberry jam, frozen raspberries, and raspberry sherbet for strawberry jam, strawberries, and strawberry yogurt.

 Smooth Sailing

Want your kids to drink their milk? Try adding a little fruit-flavored jam to it. A good ratio is 2 tablespoons per cup of milk, and most kids like it better if you use puréed jelly so there are no pieces.

Caramel Walnut Smoothie

Prep time: less than 10 minutes • Makes: 2 (15-ounce) servings

Each serving has: 673 calories • 283 calories from fat • 31½ g fat
• 9 g saturated fat • 16 g protein • 89 g carbohydrates

1 cup milk

½ cup walnut ice cream topping

½ cup caramel sauce

½ cup walnuts

½ tsp. ground cinnamon

1½ cups vanilla frozen yogurt or ice cream

Smooth Sailing

You can make your own walnut ice cream topping easily by combining two parts sugar to one part water and bringing it to a simmer. Then stir in the toasted walnuts.

Combine milk, walnut topping, caramel sauce, walnuts, and cinnamon in a blender. Blend on high speed until walnuts are puréed and mixture is smooth. Add vanilla frozen yogurt and blend on high speed again until smooth. Serve immediately.

Variation: Substitute chocolate fudge sauce or butterscotch sauce for caramel sauce.

Butterscotch Apple Smoothie

Prep time: less than 10 minutes   •   Makes: 2 (15-ounce) servings

Each serving has: 553 calories   •   72 calories from fat   •   8 g fat   •
4½ g saturated fat   •   5 g protein   •   123 g carbohydrates

1 cup applesauce

¾ cup chilled *butterscotch* sauce

1 sweet eating apple, such as
McIntosh, Jonathan, or York
Imperial, peeled, cored, and diced

½ tsp. ground cinnamon

1 cup vanilla frozen yogurt or ice
cream

Combine applesauce, butterscotch
sauce, apple, and cinnamon in a
blender. Blend on high speed until
apple is puréed and mixture is
smooth. Add vanilla frozen yogurt
and blend on high speed again until
smooth. Serve immediately.

Variation: Substitute caramel sauce
for butterscotch sauce.

Ellen on Edibles

Butterscotch is a
blending of butter with brown
sugar. The mixture is usually
cooked until the sugar melts
and releases its molasses.

Banana Nut Smoothie

Prep time: less than 10 minutes • Makes: 2 (15-ounce) servings

Each serving has: 511 calories • 261 calories from fat • 29 g fat •
7 g saturated fat • 10 g protein • 58 g carbohydrates

1 cup milk

2 large bananas, peeled and sliced

½ tsp. pure vanilla extract

½ cup toasted pecans

1 cup butter-pecan ice cream

Blender Beware

Ice creams such as butter pecan and cherry vanilla contain a large percentage of frozen solids. Allow the blender to run for at least 30 seconds to ensure the solids have been properly pulverized.

Combine milk, bananas, vanilla extract, and pecans in a blender. Blend on high speed until nuts are puréed and mixture is smooth. Add butter pecan ice cream and blend on high speed again until nuts are puréed and mixture is smooth. Serve immediately.

Variation: Substitute walnuts and vanilla frozen yogurt or ice cream for pecans and butter pecan ice cream.

Triple Cherry Smoothie

Prep time: less than 10 minutes • Makes: 2 (15-ounce) servings

Each serving has: 380 calories • 95 calories from fat • 10½ g fat • 5 g saturated fat • 8 g protein • 61 g carbohydrates

1 cup milk

1 (8-oz.) container cherry low-fat yogurt

¼ tsp. pure vanilla extract

1½ cups frozen, pitted cherries

1 cup cherry-vanilla ice cream

Combine milk, cherry yogurt, vanilla extract, and cherries in a blender. Blend on high speed until cherries are puréed and mixture is smooth. Add cherry-vanilla ice cream and blend on high speed again until fruit in ice cream is puréed and mixture is smooth. Serve immediately.

Variation: Substitute strawberry yogurt, frozen strawberries, and strawberry ice cream for cherry yogurt, cherries, and cherry-vanilla ice cream.

 Smooth Sailing

It's easy to make substitutions for specialized ice cream. For cherry vanilla, add an additional ¼ cup cherries for each ½ cup vanilla ice cream. For chocolate chip, add the same proportion of chocolate chips.

Carrot Cake Smoothie

Prep time: less than 10 minutes • Makes: 2 (15-ounce) servings

Each serving has: 513 calories • 288 calories from fat • 32 g fat • 12 g saturated fat • 12 g protein • 51 g carbohydrates

1 cup chilled carrot juice

½ cup shredded coconut

½ cup toasted walnuts

½ tsp. ground cinnamon

1 cup frozen diced pineapple

1 cup vanilla frozen yogurt or ice cream

Smooth Sailing

If you have carrots but no carrot juice, combine ½ cup water and 1 large carrot, scrubbed and sliced, in the blender and purée the mixture before adding any other ingredients.

Combine carrot juice, coconut, walnuts, cinnamon, and pineapple in a blender. Blend on high speed until nuts and pineapple are puréed and mixture is smooth. Add vanilla frozen yogurt and blend on high speed again until smooth. Serve immediately.

Variation: Substitute pecans or almonds for walnuts.

Creamy Sesame Smoothie

Prep time: less than 10 minutes • Makes: 2 (15-ounce) servings

Each serving has: 846 calories • 414 calories from fat • 46 g fat • 13 g saturated fat • 23 g protein • 94 g carbohydrates

1 cup chilled milk

1 cup vanilla *halvah*, broken into pieces

¼ cup tahini

½ tsp. pure vanilla extract

1½ cups vanilla frozen yogurt or ice cream

Combine milk, halvah, tahini, and vanilla extract in a blender. Blend on high speed until mixture is smooth. Add vanilla frozen yogurt and blend on high speed again until smooth. Serve immediately.

Variation: Substitute chocolate milk and chocolate frozen yogurt or ice cream for plain milk and vanilla frozen yogurt.

Ellen on Edibles

Halvah is a Middle Eastern candy made from ground sesame seeds and honey, sometimes with the addition of chocolate marbling or pistachio nuts. It's sold both in bars and in bulk in the delicatessen sections of most supermarkets.

Fig and Cookie Smoothie

Prep time: less than 10 minutes • Makes: 2 (15-ounce) servings

Each serving has: 713 calories • 180 calories from fat • 20 g fat • 8½ g saturated fat • 14 g protein • 124 g carbohydrates

1½ cups milk

1 cup dried figs, preferably unsulfured, diced

1 cup crushed sugar cookies

1 cup vanilla frozen yogurt or ice cream

Blender Beware

Dried fruit such as figs and prunes frequently have the tough, woody stems still attached. Be sure to discard these because they will never pulverize in the blender.

Combine milk, figs, and crushed cookies in a blender. Blend on high speed until figs are puréed and mixture is smooth. Add vanilla frozen yogurt and blend on high speed again until smooth. Serve immediately.

Variation: Substitute dried apricots or raisins, unsulfured if possible, for dried figs.

Maple Pecan Smoothie

Prep time: less than 10 minutes • Makes: 2 (15-ounce) servings

Each serving has: 789 calories • 436 calories from fat • 48½ g fat • 8½ g saturated fat • 11 g protein • 86 g carbohydrates

1 cup milk

½ cup pure maple syrup

1 cup toasted pecans

1 cup butter pecan ice cream

Combine milk, maple syrup, and pecans in a blender. Blend on high speed until pecans are puréed and mixture is smooth. Add butter pecan ice cream and blend on high speed again until pecans are puréed and mixture is smooth. Serve immediately.

Variation: Substitute walnuts and vanilla ice cream for pecans and butter pecan ice cream.

Smooth Sailing

You can always use maple sugar in place of maple syrup in a recipe. Be sure to melt the sugar with a few tablespoons water in the microwave or in a small saucepan before adding it to the recipe.

Chapter **14**

Tipsy Sippers

In This Chapter

- ◆ Wine-based smoothies
- ◆ Creamy frozen-yogurt and ice-cream cocktails
- ◆ After-dinner smoothies

This is the "adult only" chapter, so if you're under the legal drinking age for your state, please go to another chapter. Or if you peek anyway, please imagine the flavors without sampling them.

Sweet drinks have always been popular for both before and after dinner, and you can serve the recipes in this chapter at either time. Or use them as an adult dessert served in a glass. Many of them contain rum, as the tropics have been the launching pad of many famous rum-laced concoctions since the tourist industry began.

Some of these drinks, like the Piña Colada Smoothie and the Grasshopper Smoothie, are thicker versions of classic cocktails. Others are ones that might join their ranks.

Dessert smoothies are great to garnish, should you be industrious.

Citrus Red Wine Smoothie

Prep time: less than 10 minutes   •   Makes: 2 (8-ounce) servings

Each serving has: 279 calories   •   0 calories from fat   •   0 g fat   •
0 g saturated fat   •   1 g protein   •   33 g carbohydrates

1 cup chilled red wine

¼ cup orange juice

¼ cup *triple sec*

2 frozen, peeled, pith removed, and diced oranges

¼ cup lemon sorbet

Ellen on Edibles

Triple sec is a clear liqueur with a strong orange flavor. It is similar to Curaçao, and it is known by the brand name of Conintreau.

Combine red wine, orange juice, triple sec, oranges, and sorbet in a blender. Blend on high speed until oranges are puréed and mixture is smooth. Serve immediately.

Variation: Substitute white wine for red wine.

Peach and Champagne Smoothie

Prep time: less than 10 minutes • Makes: 2 (8-ounce) servings

Each serving has: 165 calories • 0 calories from fat • 0 g fat • 0 g saturated fat • ½ g protein • 12 g carbohydrates

| 1 cup chilled Champagne or sparkling wine | 1 frozen, peeled, sliced large peach or ¾ cup frozen peach slices |

2 TB. peach liqueur

Combine Champagne, peach liqueur, and peaches in a blender. Blend on high speed until peaches are puréed and mixture is smooth. Serve immediately.

Variation: To make the drink more like a mimosa, substitute triple sec and 2 frozen oranges for peach liqueur and peach.

Smooth Sailing

You can buy specialized caps to preserve the bubbles in sparkling wines, but you can also do this by dangling a silver fork into the bottle; it's not necessary for it to touch the remaining wine. I didn't believe this worked, but I tried it and it does!

Pineapple Apricot Smoothie

Prep time: less than 10 minutes • Makes: 2 (8-ounce) servings

Each serving has: 333 calories • 0 calories from fat • 0 g fat • 0 g saturated fat • 1 g protein • 51 carbohydrates

¼ cup chilled light rum

¼ cup chilled apricot brandy

½ cup diced fresh apricots

1 cup pineapple sorbet

Combine rum, apricot brandy, and apricots in a blender. Blend on high speed until apricots are puréed and mixture is smooth. Add pineapple sorbet and blend on high speed again until smooth. Serve immediately.

Variation: Substitute fresh pineapple for pineapple sorbet.

Smooth Sailing

Sorbets are merely fruit, water, and possibly sugar, and you can use fresh or frozen fruit as a substitute. For tart sorbets such as lemon or lime, add superfine sugar, to taste, as well.

Coconut Strawberry Smoothie

Prep time: less than 10 minutes   •   Makes: 2 (8-ounce) servings

Each serving has: 367 calories   •   144 calories from fat   •   16 g fat   •
15 g saturated fat   •   2 g protein   •   31 g carbohydrates

½ cup chilled, canned coconut milk

½ cup chilled *coconut rum*

½ cup frozen strawberries

½ cup strawberry ice cream

Combine coconut milk, coconut rum, strawberries, and strawberry ice cream in a blender. Blend on high speed until strawberries are puréed and mixture is smooth. Serve immediately.

Variation: Substitute frozen raspberries and raspberry sherbet for strawberries and strawberry ice cream.

Ellen on Edibles

Coconut rum is a light rum that has coconut meat added during the distillation process. The coconut is then strained out, but its flavor is prominent in the bottle.

Low-Carb Rum Smoothie

Prep time: less than 10 minutes   •   Makes: 2 (8-ounce) servings

Each serving has: 168 calories   •   0 calories from fat   •   0 g fat   •
0 g saturated fat   •   1 g protein   •   7 g carbohydrates

1 cup chilled double-strength
no-calorie pineapple and orange
fruit drink, such as Crystal Light

½ cup chilled dark rum

1 cup frozen diced papaya

4 ice cubes

Combine fruit drink, rum, papaya, and ice cubes in a blender. Blend
on high speed until papaya is puréed and mixture is smooth. Serve
immediately.

Variation: Use any no-calorie tropical fruit drink, or substitute mango for
papaya.

Smooth Sailing

Refined sugar is what adds empty carbohydrate grams to any
drink or recipe. Rum (and vodka, too) has no carbohydrates, so it's
a carb-watcher's best friend at cocktail hour.

Piña Colada Smoothie

Prep time: less than 10 minutes • Makes: 2 (8-ounce) servings

Each serving has: 244 calories • 18 calories from fat • 2 g fat • 2 g saturated fat • <1 g protein • 21 g carbohydrates

½ cup chilled *cream of coconut*

½ cup chilled light rum

1 cup frozen, diced pineapple

Combine cream of coconut, rum, and pineapple in a blender. Blend on high speed until pineapple is puréed and mixture is smooth. Serve immediately.

Variation: Substitute dark rum or coconut rum for light rum. Use pineapple sorbet in place of diced pineapple.

Ellen on Edibles

Cream of coconut is a very highly sweetened coconut milk made in Central America. Only use it in drinks and desserts, and never substitute it for coconut milk in a recipe.

Bananas Foster Smoothie

Prep time: less than 10 minutes • Makes: 2 (8-ounce) servings

Each serving has: 441 calories • 54 calories from fat • 6 g fat • 4 g saturated fat • 3 g protein • 55 g carbohydrates

¼ cup chilled dark rum

¼ cup chilled *crème de banana*

¼ cup firmly packed dark brown sugar

¼ tsp. ground cinnamon

1 frozen, sliced large banana

¾ cup vanilla frozen yogurt or ice cream

Ellen on Edibles

Crème de banana is a liqueur distilled with fresh bananas. If you can't find it, skip this recipe because there's no substitute for it.

Combine rum, crème de banana, brown sugar, and cinnamon in a blender. Blend on high speed until mixture is smooth. Add banana and vanilla frozen yogurt, and blend on high speed until banana is puréed and mixture is smooth. Serve immediately.

Variation: Substitute banana frozen yogurt or butter pecan ice cream for vanilla frozen yogurt.

Strawberry Margarita Smoothie

Prep time: less than 10 minutes • Makes: 2 (8-ounce) servings

Each serving has: 214 calories • 0 calories from fat • 0 g fat •
0 g saturated fat • 1 g protein • 18 g carbohydrates

⅓ cup chilled tequila

¼ cup chilled *crème de cassis*

2 TB. lime juice

1 cup frozen strawberries

4 ice cubes

Combine tequila, crème de cassis, lime juice, and strawberries in a blender. Blend on high speed until strawberries are puréed and mixture is smooth. Add ice cubes and blend on high speed until smooth. Serve immediately.

Variation: Substitute raspberries for strawberries.

Ellen on Edibles

Crème de cassis is a very sweet liqueur with a black currant flavor. A few drops of it are added to white wine for a *kir* cocktail, or to sparkling wine for a *kir royale* cocktail.

Banana Daiquiri Smoothie

Prep time: less than 10 minutes • Makes: 2 (8-ounce) servings

Each serving has: 260 calories • 0 calories from fat • 0 g fat • 0 g saturated fat • 1 g protein • 30 g carbohydrates

½ cup chilled light rum

2 TB. lime juice

2 TB. *simple syrup*

1 frozen, sliced large banana

4 ice cubes

Combine rum, lime juice, simple syrup, and banana in a blender. Blend on high speed until banana is puréed and mixture is smooth. Add ice cubes and blend on high speed again until smooth. Serve immediately.

Variation: Substitute 1 cup frozen strawberries or raspberries for banana.

Ellen on Edibles

Simple syrup is a combination of two parts granulated sugar to one part water that is heated over low heat until the sugar dissolves and the mixture is clear. Use it to sweeten cold drinks because regular sugar might remain gritty.

Brandy Alexander Smoothie

Prep time: less than 10 minutes • Makes: 2 (8-ounce) servings

Each serving has: 434 calories • 63 calories from fat • 7 g fat • 5 g saturated fat • 6 g protein • 54 g carbohydrates

¼ cup chilled brandy

¼ cup chilled crème de cacao (clear chocolate liqueur)

2 TB. coffee syrup, found in super-markets with chocolate syrup

1½ cups vanilla frozen yogurt or ice cream

Combine brandy, crème de cacao, coffee syrup, and vanilla frozen yogurt in a blender. Blend on high speed until mixture is smooth. Serve immediately.

Variation: For a chocolate-flavored drink, substitute chocolate syrup and chocolate frozen yogurt or ice cream for coffee syrup and vanilla frozen yogurt.

Blender Beware

When adding frozen yogurt or ice cream to a blender, always be sure the scoops are not larger than ½ cup. Any larger scoop might get stuck on the blades and make the blender work too hard.

Mango Orange Smoothie

Prep time: less than 10 minutes • Makes: 2 (8-ounce) servings

Each serving has: 267 calories • 9 calories from fat • 1 g fat • ½ g saturated fat • 1 g protein • 33 g carbohydrates

½ cup chilled triple sec or other orange liqueur

2 TB. lemon juice

1 cup frozen, diced mango

½ cup orange sherbet

Smooth Sailing

The easiest way to squeeze lemons for fresh lemon juice is to hold a lemon half in one hand and squeeze the juice right through your fingers. Toss the seeds, and there's no squeezer or bowl to wash.

Combine triple sec, lemon juice, and mango in a blender. Blend on high speed until mango is puréed and mixture is smooth. Add sherbet and blend on high speed until smooth. Serve immediately.

Variation: Substitute papaya for mango. For a dairy-free drink, use sorbet instead of sherbet.

Peach and Banana Smoothie

Prep time: less than 10 minutes • Makes: 2 (8-ounce) servings

Each serving has: 239 calories • 0 calories from fat • 0 g fat • 0 g saturated fat • 2 g protein • 43 g carbohydrates

¼ cup chilled peach brandy

¼ cup chilled crème de banana

1 large peach, peeled and sliced, or ¾ cup frozen peach slices

1 frozen, sliced, small banana

Combine peach brandy, crème de banana, and peach in a blender. Blend on high speed until peach is puréed and mixture is smooth. Add banana and blend on high speed again until smooth. Serve immediately.

Variation: Substitute apricot brandy and diced fresh apricots for peach brandy and peaches.

 Smooth Sailing

If you're using frozen peach slices, include a room-temperature banana rather than a frozen one. Too many frozen ingredients can make your smoothie too thick.

Grasshopper Smoothie

Prep time: less than 10 minutes • Makes: 2 (8-ounce) servings

Each serving has: 441 calories • 126 calories from fat • 14 g fat • 9 g saturated fat • 8 g protein • 50 g carbohydrates

½ cup chilled half-and-half

¼ cup chilled green crème de menthe (a mint-flavored liqueur)

¼ cup chilled white crème de cacao

1 cup vanilla frozen yogurt or ice cream

Blender Beware

To get the pale green color of this drink, use white (clear) crème de cacao, not the brown version, which turns the drink sort of muddy-looking.

Combine half-and-half, crème de menthe, crème de cacao, and vanilla frozen yogurt in a blender. Blend on high speed until mixture is smooth. Serve immediately.

Variation: Substitute mint chocolate-chip ice cream for vanilla frozen yogurt.

Irish Coffee Smoothie

Prep time: less than 10 minutes • Makes: 2 (8-ounce) servings

Each serving has: 307 calories • 108 calories from fat • 12 g fat • 7 g saturated fat • 2 g protein • 24 g carbohydrates

½ cup chilled strong brewed coffee

¼ cup chilled *Irish whiskey*

¼ cup chilled Irish whiskey cream liqueur, such as Bailey's

1 cup coffee ice cream

Combine coffee, Irish whiskey, Irish whiskey cream liqueur, and ice cream in a blender. Blend on high speed until mixture is smooth. Serve immediately.

Variation: If you want a more boldly flavored drink, skip the Irish whiskey cream liqueur and double the amount of Irish whiskey.

Ellen on Edibles

Irish whiskey is a single-malt whiskey with a smoky, almost peatlike flavor. You can substitute Scotch whisky, but it has a very different flavor.

Amaretto Smoothie

Prep time: less than 10 minutes • Makes: 2 (8-ounce) servings

Each serving has: 475 calories • 103 calories from fat • 11½ g fat
• 5½ g saturated fat • 4 g protein • 71 g carbohydrates

½ cup chilled amaretto

½ cup crushed amaretto cookies

1 cup vanilla frozen yogurt or ice cream

Blender Beware

When using cookies in a smoothie recipe, always be sure they're crushed into pieces no larger than ½ inch, or they won't pulverize well in the blender.

Combine amaretto, crushed cookies, and vanilla frozen yogurt in a blender. Blend on high speed until mixture is smooth. Serve immediately.

Variation: Substitute sugar cookies for crushed amaretto cookies. Add ¼ teaspoon pure almond extract along with cookies.

Raspberry Chambord Smoothie

Prep time: less than 10 minutes • Makes: 2 (8-ounce) servings

Each serving has: 225 calories • 18 calories from fat • 2 g fat • 1 g saturated fat • 1 g protein • 17 g carbohydrates

½ cup chilled cranberry juice

¼ cup chilled raspberry-flavored liqueur, such as Chambord

¼ cup chilled vodka

½ cup frozen raspberries

Combine cranberry juice, raspberry-flavored liqueur, vodka, and raspberries in a blender. Blend on high speed until raspberries are puréed and mixture is smooth. Serve immediately.

Variation: Substitute crème de cassis and frozen strawberries or blackberries for raspberry liqueur and raspberries.

 Smooth Sailing

Most fruit-flavored liqueurs such as Chambord or crème de cassis are extremely sweet, so a little goes a long way. That's why vodka, which has no innate flavor of its own, is a good companion in drinks.

Appendix A

Glossary

accoutrement   An accompaniment, trapping, or garnish.

acidophilus   A friendly bacteria used to thicken yogurt that can prevent intestinal infections.

allspice   Named for its flavor echoes of several spices (cinnamon, cloves, nutmeg), allspice is used in many desserts and in rich marinades and stews.

almonds   Mild, sweet, and crunchy nuts that combine nicely with mildly flavored food items.

amaretto   A popular, sweet almond liqueur from Italy.

balsamic vinegar   Vinegar produced primarily in Italy from a specific type of grape and aged in wood barrels. It is heavier, darker, and sweeter than most vinegars.

basil   A flavorful, almost sweet, resinous herb delicious with tomatoes and in all kinds of Italian or Mediterranean-style dishes. Other varieties are used in Asian, especially Thai, cooking.

bee pollen   A protein-rich honey by-product made from the seeds of flower blossoms.

binder   An ingredient such as egg yolks or a mixture of flour and liquid that makes a dish thick.

blend To completely mix something, usually with a blender or food processor, more slowly than beating.

boil To heat a liquid to a point where water is forced to turn into steam, causing the liquid to bubble. To boil something is to insert it into boiling water. A rapid boil is when a lot of bubbles form on the surface of the liquid.

butterscotch A candy or sauce made by blending brown sugar and butter.

cappuccino A coffee drink consisting of equal parts espresso and steamed milk topped with milk foam.

caramelize To cook sugar over low heat until it becomes a viscous liquid and develops a sweet caramel flavor.

cashew nuts Kidney-shaped nuts with a rich, sweet flavor that are very high in magnesium.

chai A spiced tea that originated in India. It is made with cinnamon, cardamom, cloves, pepper, and nutmeg.

chili peppers (also **chile peppers**) Any one of many different "hot" peppers, ranging in intensity from the relatively mild ancho pepper to the blisteringly hot habanero.

chives A member of the onion family, chives are found at the grocery store as bunches of very thin, long leaves that resemble tall grass. They provide an easy onion flavor to any dish.

chop To cut into pieces, usually qualified by an adverb such as "*coarsely* chopped," or by a size measurement such as "chopped into ½-inch pieces." "Finely chopped" is much closer to "minced."

chutney A spicy sweet and sour condiment that originated on the Indian subcontinent. It is made with sugar, vinegar, fruits or vegetables, and spices.

cilantro A member of the parsley family used in Mexican cooking and some Asian dishes. Cilantro is what gives some salsas their unique flavor. Use in moderation, as the flavor can overwhelm.

cinnamon A sweet, rich, aromatic spice commonly used in baking or desserts. Cinnamon can also be used for delicious and interesting entrées, and is part of many Indian curries and Middle Eastern dishes. Cinnamon is ground from the bark of a tropical tree, and cassia, a related plant, is frequently sold as cinnamon.

clementines A seedless citrus fruit with thin skin from the Mandarin orange family.

cloves A sweet, strong, almost wintergreen-flavor spice used in baking and with meats such as ham.

coconut milk A canned liquid produced by mixing boiling water with grated coconut meat and straining out the solids to produce a "milk." It is high in calories and fat unless you use the "light" variety.

coconut rum A light rum that has coconut meat added during the distillation process. The coconut is then strained out, but its flavor is prominent in the bottle.

cola nut A tropical nut that contains a large amount of caffeine. It's a main ingredient in many soft drinks.

complete protein A component of certain foods that contains all the essential amino acids in the appropriate proportions. Foods such as meats and soy products contain complete proteins. Other foods, such as beans and grains, contain incomplete proteins but can be combined to make complete proteins.

core As a verb, it means to remove the unappetizing middle membranes and seeds of fruits and vegetables. As a noun, it is the seeds and membranes of certain fruits and vegetables.

coriander seed A rich, warm spice used in all types of recipes, from African to Indian to South American, from entrées to desserts. The green leaf of the same plant is known as cilantro or Chinese coriander.

cream of coconut A highly sweetened coconut milk used for drinks and desserts.

crème de banana A distilled liqueur made with fresh bananas.

crème de cassis A sweet liqueur made from black currants used in small quantities to make cocktails.

crystallized ginger   Dried fresh diced ginger candied in a sugar syrup to preserve it.

dash   A dash refers to a few drops, usually of a liquid, that is released by a quick shake of, for example, a bottle of hot sauce.

dice   To cut into small cubes about ¼-inch square.

dill   An herb with a feathery leaf. Fresh-tasting, aromatic herb used in all Scandinavian and many other European cuisines. The seeds of the same plant are often used for brining pickles.

dry-packed   The way fruit is described when frozen in individual pieces without additional sugar or in a syrup.

emulsion   A combination of two distinct ingredients that are blended together to form a new mixture. Classic examples are salad dressings and mayonnaise. Creation of an emulsion must be done carefully and rapidly to ensure that particles of one ingredient are suspended in the other.

espresso   Strong coffee made by forcing steam through finely ground coffee beans.

extract   A liquid with flavor highly concentrated by distillation or evaporation.

flaxseed   A small seed with a nutty flavor that contains omega-3 fatty acids.

floret   The flower or bud end of broccoli or cauliflower.

frais du bois   Tiny French strawberries with a very intense flavor.

garlic   A member of the onion family, a pungent and flavorful element in many savory dishes. A garlic bulb, the form in which garlic is often sold, contains multiple cloves. Each clove, when chopped, provides about 1 teaspoon.

garnish   An embellishment not vital to the dish, but added to enhance visual appeal.

ginger   A rhizome that is available in fresh or powdered form, ginger adds a pungent, sweet, and spicy quality to a dish. It is a very popular element of many Asian and Indian dishes, and in Euro-American baking among others. Crystallized ginger is dried fresh, diced ginger candied in a sugar syrup to preserve it.

grate To shave into tiny pieces using a sharp rasp or grater.

grind To reduce a solid substance to a powder or small pieces.

halvah A Middle Eastern confection made from ground sesame seeds and honey, sometimes with the addition of chocolate or nuts.

handful An unscientific measurement term that refers to the amount of an ingredient you can hold in your hand.

hazelnut (also **filbert**) A sweet nut popular in desserts and, to a lesser degree, in savory dishes.

herbs The leaves of flavorful plants characterized by fresh, pungent aromas and flavors, such as parsley, sage, rosemary, and thyme. They are used to flavor and add accent notes to many dishes.

herbes de Provence A seasoning mix including basil, fennel, marjoram, rosemary, sage, and thyme. It originated in the French province of Provençe.

honey A sweet, thick liquid made by bees from various flower nectars. In general, the darker the color of the honey, the richer the flavor.

hors d'oeuvre French for "outside of work" (the "work" being the main meal). An hors d'oeuvre can be any dish served as a starter before the meal.

hot red pepper sauce Also called hot sauce. *See* Tabasco sauce.

infusion A liquid in which flavorful ingredients such as herbs have been soaked or steeped to extract that flavor into the liquid.

Irish whiskey A single-malt whiskey with a smoky, peatlike flavor.

julienne A French word meaning to slice into very thin pieces.

kefir Similar to yogurt but made with a different bacteria that produces a smaller curd size.

kiwi Small furry fruit that should always be peeled to reveal sweet green flesh flecked with black seeds.

latte A coffee drink with one part espresso and two parts steamed milk.

macerate   To mix sugar or another sweetener with fruit. The fruit softens, and its juice is released to mix with the sweetener.

malted milk powder   A slightly sweet powder made from malt, a grain similar to barley, used to flavor malts as well as malt vinegar.

marjoram   A sweet herb, a cousin of and similar to oregano, popular in Greek, Spanish, Italian and other dishes.

marmalade   A fruit-and-sugar preserve that contains whole pieces of fruit peel to achieve simultaneous sweetness (from the sugar) and tartness (from the fruit's natural acids). The most common marmalades are made with citrus fruits such as orange and lemon.

meld   A combination of *melt* and *weld;* many cooks use this term to describe how flavors blend and spread over time throughout dips and spreads and other dishes. Melding is often why recipes call for overnight refrigeration and is also why some dishes taste better as leftovers.

mince   To cut into very small pieces smaller than diced pieces, about ⅛ inch or smaller.

mull (or **mulled**)   To heat a liquid with the addition of spices and sometimes sweeteners.

nectar   A juice made from tree fruits such as peaches and apricots that has a thicker texture than other fruit juices.

nut   A shell-covered seed whose meat is rich in flavor and nutrition. A critical component in many dishes, many nuts are tasty on their own as well. *See also* almonds; hazelnuts; pecans; walnuts.

nutmeg   A sweet, fragrant, musky spice used primarily in baking.

oregano   A fragrant, slightly astringent herb used in Greek, Spanish, Italian, and other dishes.

oxidation   The browning of fruit flesh that happens over time and with exposure to air. If you need to cut apples in advance, minimize oxidation by rubbing the cut surfaces with a lemon half.

papain   An enzyme found in the skin of papaya used to reduce indigestion that also tenderizes meats if part of a marinade.

pare   To scrape away the skin of a food, usually a vegetable, as part of preparation for serving or cooking.

parsley   A fresh-tasting green, leafy herb used to add color, flavor, and interest to just about any savory dish. Often used to garnish a dish just before serving.

peanuts   The nutritious and high-fat seeds of the legume known as the peanut plant (a relative of the pea) that are sold shelled or unshelled and in a variety of preparations, including peanut butter and peanut oil. Some people are allergic to peanuts, so care should be taken with their inclusion in recipes.

pecans   Rich, buttery nuts native to North America. Their flavor, a terrific addition to baked goods, is at least partially due to the mouth feel created by their high unsaturated fat content.

pepper   A biting and pungent spice, freshly ground pepper is a must for many dishes and adds an extra level of flavor and taste.

peppercorns   Large, round, dried berries that are ground to produce the spice known as pepper.

pinch   An unscientific measurement term that refers to the amount of an ingredient—typically a dry, granular substance such as an herb or seasoning—you can hold between your finger and thumb.

purée   To reduce a food to a thick, creamy texture, usually using a blender or food processor.

scant   A measurement modification that specifies "include no extra," as in 1 scant teaspoon.

shred   To cut into many long, thin slices.

simple syrup   A combination of two parts granulated sugar to one part water, heated until the liquid is clear and the sugar is dissolved.

slice   To cut into thin pieces.

sorbet   A fruit-flavored ice made without the addition of any dairy product.

sweetened condensed milk   A canned evaporated milk that has sugar already blended into it.

Tabasco sauce   A popular brand of Louisiana hot pepper sauce used in usually small portions to season savory food. The name also refers to a type of hot pepper from Tabasco, a state in Mexico, that is used to make this sauce.

tahini   A paste made from sesame seeds that is used to flavor many Middle Eastern recipes.

toffee   A traditional English sweet that is similar to caramel with butter added.

tofu   A substance made from soybeans and soy milk. Flavorful and nutritious, tofu is an important component of foods across the globe, especially from the Far East.

triple sec   A clear liqueur with a strong orange flavor.

twist   A twist (as in lemon or other citrus fruit) is simply an attractive way to garnish an appetizer or other dish. Cut a thin, about ⅛-inch–thick cross-section, slice of a lemon, for example. Then take that slice and cut from the center out to the edge of the slice on one side. Pick up the piece of lemon and pull apart the two cut ends in opposite directions.

unsulphered dry fruit   Dried fruit that has not been sprayed with sulphur dioxide, a gas used for fumigation, which also destroys B vitamins.

yogurt   A coagulated milk product made with friendly bacteria that cause the milk to thicken and give it a tangy, slightly astringent taste.

walnuts   Grown worldwide, walnuts bring a rich, slightly woody flavor to all types of food. For the quick cook, walnuts are available chopped and ready to go at your grocery store. They are delicious toasted and make fine accompaniments to cheeses and baked goods.

white chocolate   Similar in flavor and texture (though not color) but not truly a chocolate because it contains only cocoa butter, not chocolate liquor.

zest   Small slivers of peel, usually from a citrus fruit such as lemon, lime, or orange.

zester   A small kitchen tool used to scrape zest off a fruit. A small grater also works fine.

Metric Conversion Charts

Smoothies are very tolerant recipes. A few extra tablespoons of this or that will not influence the final result, but it's always good to measure as precisely as possible.

The charts in this appendix are designed for general cooking. If you are making conversions for baking, grab your calculator and compute the exact figure.

Even though the smoothies do not require cooking, a temperature conversion chart is included to make this appendix your basic metric reference. Bookmark this appendix or photocopy the pages and post them inside a cupboard door for easy access.

Converting Ounces to Grams

The numbers in the following table are approximate. To reach the exact amount of grams, multiply the number of ounces by 28.35.

Ounces	Grams
1 oz.	30 g
2 oz.	60 g
3 oz.	85 g
4 oz.	115 g
5 oz.	140 g
6 oz.	180 g
7 oz.	200 g
8 oz.	225 g
9 oz.	250 g
10 oz.	285 g
11 oz.	300 g
12 oz.	340 g
13 oz.	370 g
14 oz.	400 g
15 oz.	425 g
16 oz.	450 g

Converting Quarts to Liters

The numbers in the following table are approximate. To reach the exact amount of liters, multiply the number of quarts by 0.95.

Quarts	Liters
1 cup (¼ qt.)	¼ L
1 pint (½ qt.)	½ L
1 qt.	1 L
2 qt.	2 L

Quarts	Liters
2½ qt.	2½ L
3 qt.	2¾ L
4 qt.	3¾ L
5 qt.	4¾ L
6 qt.	5½ L
7 qt.	6½ L
8 qt.	7½ L

Converting Pounds to Grams and Kilograms

The numbers in the following table are approximate. To reach the exact amount of kilograms, multiply the number of pounds by 453.6.

Pounds	Grams; Kilograms
1 lb.	450 g
1½ lb.	675 g
2 lb.	900 g
2½ lb.	1,125 g; 1¼ kg
3 lb.	1,350 g
3½ lb.	1,500 g; 1½ kg
4 lb.	1,800 g
4½ lb.	2 kg
5 lb.	2¼ kg
5½ lb.	2½ kg
6 lb.	2¾ kg
6½ lb.	3 kg
7 lb.	3¼ kg
7½ lb.	3½ kg
8 lb.	3¾ kg

Converting Fahrenheit to Celsius

The numbers in the following table are approximate. To reach the exact temperature, subtract 32 from the Fahrenheit reading, multiply the number by 5, then divide by 9.

Fahrenheit	Celsius
170°F	77°C
180°F	82°C
190°F	88°C
200°F	95°C
225°F	110°C
250°F	120°C
300°F	150°C
325°F	165°C
350°F	180°C
375°F	190°C
400°F	205°C
425°F	220°C
450°F	230°C
475°F	245°C
500°F	260°C

Converting Inches to Centimeters

The numbers in the following table are approximate. To reach the exact number of centimeters, multiply the number of inches by 2.54.

Inches	Centimeters
½ in.	1.5 cm
1 in.	2.5 cm
2 in.	5 cm
3 in.	8 cm
4 in.	10 cm

Inches	Centimeters
5 in.	13 cm
6 in.	15 cm
7 in.	18 cm
8 in.	20 cm
9 in.	23 cm
10 in.	25 cm
11 in.	28 cm
12 in.	30 cm

Index

Check Out These
Best-Sellers

Read by millions!

Grammar and Style
SECOND EDITION

1-59257-115-8
$16.95

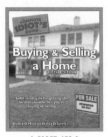

Buying & Selling a Home
FIFTH EDITION

1-59257-458-0
$19.95

Being a Groom
THIRD EDITION

1-59257-451-3
$9.95

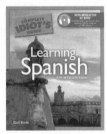

Learning Spanish
FOURTH EDITION

1-59257-485-8
$24.95

Investing
THIRD EDITION

1-59257-480-7
$19.95

Baby Sign Language

1-59257-469-6
$14.95

Total Nutrition
FOURTH EDITION

1-59257-439-4
$18.95

Positive Dog Training
SECOND EDITION

1-59257-483-1
$14.95

The Bible
THIRD EDITION

1-59257-389-4
$18.95

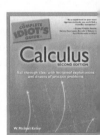

Calculus
SECOND EDITION

1-59257-471-8
$18.95

Music Theory
SECOND EDITION

1-59257-437-8
$19.95

The Perfect Resume
FOURTH EDITION

1-59257-463-7
$14.95

Playing the Guitar
SECOND EDITION

0-02-864244-9
$21.95

Manga Illustrated

1-59257-335-5
$19.95

Knitting & Crocheting
THIRD EDITION
Illustrated

1-59257-491-2
$16.95

More than *450 titles* available at booksellers and online retailers everywhere

www.idiotsguides.com

ALPH